Crochet
ANIMAL
BLANKETS AND BLOCKS
· · · · · · · · · · · · · · · ·

Ira Rott

DAVID & CHARLES

www.davidandcharles.com

Contents

· · · · · · · · · · ·

Welcome!

. . . .

Hello and welcome to the world of crochet animals! Get your yarn and hooks ready to dive into your happy place, making fun crochet projects for your family and friends.

This book features 18 animal blocks with fun 3D elements. You can incorporate them into several different projects, such as blankets, cushion covers, a toy storage bag, or a book bag and backpack. You can even use each block individually as a wall hanging or a doll blanket.

To inspire imagination, you can mix and match elements from different animal blocks, creating your own animal variations. For example, make a Horse using Unicorn, Bunny and Dog, or make a Bear using Sloth, Bunny and Lion (see Additional Ideas).

Finish a blanket using your favorite animal design or combine different blocks to make your projects fun and colorful. For a woodland theme, use the Fox, Raccoon, Bunny and Bear blocks. For a farm blanket, use the Pig, Cow, Sheep, Cat and Horse. Turn your room into a jungle with a cheerful blanket made from the Hippo, Monkey and Lion blocks. While the possibilities are endless, you may want to make 16 different animals and join them into a large 4 x 4 blocks blanket.

If you are not familiar with the stitches or techniques used in this book, be sure to check the Techniques section when you work on your projects. I've included many tips and tricks along the way as well. Be happy and keep crafting!

Ira Rott

Happy Crafting!

How to Use this Book

SKILL LEVELS

All animal blocks and projects in this book have been assigned a level of difficulty based on the crochet stitches and techniques used for creating these designs – Easy (1), Moderate (2) and Challenging (3). Pick a pattern that suits your skill level, and then move up to the next level as you get more comfortable with your projects.

EASY – Best choice for confident beginners. These patterns include basic and reverse crochet stitches, with simple repeats and easy assembly. Graphic elements in colorwork have simple shapes, with only 3 color sections per row.

MODERATE – These patterns have basic stitches, as well as some unique, yet easy to learn stitches: front post and back post stitches, popcorn stitch and picot. Assembling details may include more intricate sewing. Graphic elements in colorwork do not exceed 3 color sections per row.

CHALLENGING – Graphic elements in colorwork are more complex, with up to 7 color sections per row. Some patterns include loop stitch and crossed double crochet stitch. Sewing details could be more challenging in patterns with loop stitches.

READING PATTERNS

Crochet patterns in this book are written using American (US) terminology. If you are accustomed to British terminology, you can convert the terms using our conversion chart (see Useful Information: Terminology).

- "Work in rows" means – Crochet a row of stitches, then turn your work to begin the next row. The patterns will specify which rows are right side (RS) or wrong side (WS) when this extra information is helpful or important.
- "Work in the round" means – Begin with a magic ring/foundation ring or work along both sides of the foundation chain. Work with right side (RS) facing you, joining each round with a slip stitch in top of the beginning stitch.
- "Work in spiral rounds" means – Begin with a magic ring/foundation ring. With right side (RS) facing, work the beginning stitch of each round into the first stitch of the previous round without joining. This creates a continuous spiral appearance of the rounds.

The total stitch count is indicated after the equal sign (=) at the end of each row/round. The beginning chain(s) might be counted as stitch(es) or not, as marked at the beginning of the rows/rounds. Some instructions apply to multiple rows/rounds. Example: Ch 2 (counts as dc now and throughout).

READING CHARTS

A crochet chart is an illustration that uses symbols to represent stitches which helps you visualize patterns. The beginning of the work in the charts is marked with a small black arrow, and each row/round is marked with a number. Different colors indicate yarn colors. To understand a chart, refer to the symbol key (see Useful Information: Abbreviations). You can choose to follow a chart or a written pattern, or even use both. The charts shown in this book are for right-handed crochet and show your work on the right side (RS). Some charts may begin or end on the wrong side (WS).

GAUGE

Since crochet tension varies from person to person, it's important to test and achieve the gauge of the pattern for accurate sizing and yarn requirements.

So what is the gauge? The gauge is a given number of stitches and rows per 4 x 4in (10 x 10cm) square, which regulates the size of your finished animal blocks. If you crochet too tightly, your blocks will turn out smaller and you will have yarn leftovers, but if you crochet too loosely, your blocks will be bigger and you may run out of yarn before you finish your project.

To test your gauge, make a swatch slightly larger than indicated, so you can comfortably measure it. Using a regular ruler or a gauge tool, simply measure and count the rows and stitches in your swatch, then compare your results to the gauge numbers provided in the pattern. You can use a larger or smaller size hook to obtain the gauge if necessary. Once you've calibrated the gauge, it's important to keep it consistent as it will be hard to join your blocks if they vary in size. It's good practice to measure your stitches once in a while along the way to ensure consistency.

Tip

The yarn requirements provided for each animal block include a small amount of overage to ensure you have enough yarn for your project. However, you might need more or less yarn if your gauge is different. You will also need additional yarn to make some of the projects.

PROJECTS

The animal patterns in this book indicate how much yarn you will need to complete 1 block, 4 blocks for a Small Blanket, 9 blocks for a Medium Blanket, and 16 blocks for a Large Blanket.

There are several different project ideas that you can make using these blocks: blankets with different borders in small, medium and large sizes; a cushion cover with alteration tips for different sizes; a toy storage bag; a book bag and backpack; a wall hanging and doll blanket. These projects include yarn requirements that you will need in addition to the materials listed for each animal block.

To begin, pick a project you wish to make (see Project Ideas). Then choose animal designs and yarn. Make a swatch to test your gauge and have fun!

Tools and Materials

YARN

To make the projects featured in this book, I used 100% premium acrylic worsted weight yarns (Medium/4) – Red Heart Super Saver, Bernat Super Value and Bernat Premium. These yarns are soft, durable and washable, which is a wonderful choice for children's projects. You can simply follow the care instructions on the yarn labels to wash these items.

Yarn weight is the thickness of the yarn, which may vary from country to country. Use the following conversion chart if you need to find an alternative acrylic yarn based on the yarn standards in your region. When choosing your yarn, consider the fact that if the fiber content is different, the amounts of yarns suggested for each project may also vary.

US	UK	Australia	Meters per 100g	Other Terms
Medium (4)	Aran	10 ply	150-200	Worsted

CROCHET HOOKS

You will be using the same size of hook for all projects in this book – 5mm (H). However, if you need to adjust your tension to meet the gauge indicated in the patterns, you might need to use a smaller or larger size hook – 4.25mm (G) or 5.5mm (I). Here is a quick reference for hook sizes in different regions.

Metric	US Letter	US Number	Canada/UK
4.25mm/4.5mm	G	6/7	7
5mm	H	8	6
5.5mm	I	9	5

OTHER EQUIPMENT

You'll also need the following additional supplies to complete some of the blocks and projects:

- Stitch markers – for marking stitches and indicating the beginning of the rows/rounds
- Tapestry needle – for sewing elements and weaving in the ends
- Pillow form insert or cushion for cushion cover – 20 x 20in (51 x 51cm)
- 10 toggle buttons for cushion cover (optional) – 1½in (38mm)
- Wooden or bamboo dowel rod for wall hanging – ⅝ x 18in (1.5 x 45.5cm)
- Gauge tool or ruler
- Scissors

Penguin Block

· · · · · · · · · · · · ·

Keep your huddle warm and cozy under a cute penguin blanket or make a few smaller projects to surprise everyone on your gift list. Make your Penguin project even more fun by using different background colors.

MATERIALS

To make this block, use your favorite medium weight acrylic yarn (weight 4) and a 5mm (H) hook or any hook size needed to obtain the gauge (see Tools and Materials). Use the table below to determine the amount required of each color yarn.

GAUGE

14 dc x 8.5 rows = 4 x 4in (10 x 10cm)

FINISHED MEASUREMENTS

Block without border: 12 x 15in (30.5 x 38cm)
Block with border: 15 x 18in (38 x 45.5cm)

Tip

· · · · · · · · · · · · ·

Add a smart bow tie or a pretty hair bow to your penguin to give it some extra personality! Coordinating blocks can be made using gray instead of black for some penguins.

Chart color	Color key	Color name	Yarn required for 1 block	Yarn required for 4 blocks	Yarn required for 9 blocks	Yarn required for 16 blocks
●	MC	Soft Gray or Aqua	180yd (165m)	720yd (658m)	1620yd (1481m)	2880yd (2633m)
●	CC1	Black	75yd (69m)	300yd (274m)	675yd (617m)	1200yd (1097m)
●	CC2	White	35yd (32m)	140yd (128m)	315yd (288m)	560yd (512m)
●	CC3	Teal or Aqua	15yd (14m)	60yd (55m)	135yd (123m)	240yd (220m)
●	CC4	Gold	5yd (4.5m)	20yd (18m)	45yd (41m)	80yd (73m)

Block

Work in rows using the Intarsia colorwork technique (see Special Stitches). For the background, use **MC** from a skein and wind 1 butterfly-bobbin. For the penguin head, use **CC1** from a skein.

To beg: With **MC** from skein – ch 45

Row 1: (RS) Dc in fourth ch from hook (the skipped chs count as dc), dc in each ch across; turn = 43 sts

Rows 2 – 8: Ch 2 (counts as dc now and throughout), skip first st, dc in each st across; turn = 43 sts

With RS facing, place **Marker** in the center stitch of the row just made to indicate the bottom edge of the head. Continue to work in rows, changing colors through the final stage of a stitch before color change.

Rows 9 – 18: With **MC** from skein – ch 2, skip first st, dc in next st changing to **CC1** from skein; with **CC1** – dc in next 39 sts changing to **MC** from butterfly-bobbin; with **MC** – dc in next 2 sts; turn = 43 sts

Row 19: With **MC** – ch 2, skip first st, 2 dc in next st changing to **CC1**; with **CC1** – dc2tog, dc in each st until 2 sts left before color change, dc2tog changing to **MC**; with **MC** – 2 dc in next st, dc in last st; turn = 43 sts

Rows 20 – 24: With **MC** – ch 2, skip first st, dc in each st until 1 st left before color change, 2 dc in next st changing to **CC1**; with **CC1** – dc2tog, dc in each st until 2 sts left before color change, dc2tog changing to **MC**; with **MC** – 2 dc in next st, dc in each st to the end; turn = 43 sts

Break off **CC1** and **MC** from the butterfly-bobbin, and use **MC** from the skein for the rest of the block.

Rows 25 – 32: With **MC** – ch 2, skip first st, dc in each st across; turn = 43 sts

Do not fasten off, continue to work 3 rnds of Granny Square Border.

Granny Square Border

Work in the round around the entire edge of the block using **MC**. To prevent distortion in the corners, you will be changing direction every round, so the odd rounds are always on RS and the even rounds are on WS.

Rnd 1: (RS) Work across the top edge – ch 3 (counts as dc now and throughout), 2 dc in first st, *[skip 2 sts, 3 dc in next st] 13 times, skip 2 sts, (3 dc, ch 2, 3 dc) in next sp before last st (fig 1)**; work across the side edge – [skip dc of next row, 3 dc in ch-2 sp of next row] 15 times, (3 dc, ch 2, 3 dc) in last sp; work across the bottom edge – repeat from * to **; work across the side edge – [3 dc in dc of next row, skip ch-2 sp of next row] 15 times, 3 dc in dc of last row; ch 1, hdc in top of beg ch-3 (counts as last corner sp); turn = 64 groups of 3-dc and 4 corner sps

Rnd 2: (WS) Ch 3, 2 dc in same sp, *[skip 3 sts, 3 dc in next sp] to next corner, (3 dc, ch 2, 3 dc) in corner; repeat 2 more times from *; [skip 3 sts, 3 dc in next sp] to next corner, ending in hdc sp; ch 1, hdc in top of beg ch-3 (counts as last corner sp); turn = 68 groups of 3-dc and 4 corner sps

You can join blocks as-you-go while working the next round (JAYGO) or finish Rnd 3 as described for all of the other joining methods (see Joining Blocks).

Rnd 3: (RS) Ch 3, 2 dc in same sp, *[skip 3 sts, 3 dc in next sp] to next corner, (3 dc, ch 2, 3 dc) in corner; repeat 2 more times from *; [skip 3 sts, 3 dc in next sp] to next corner, ending in hdc sp; ch 2, sl st in top of beg ch-3 = 72 groups of 3-dc and 4 corner sps

Fasten off and weave in the ends.

1

Space before last st

Block

| Place **Marker** | 10 sts dividers |

Eyes

Make 2. Work in the round with **CC1**.

To beg: Ch 3, sl st in third ch from hook to form a ring (or start with a magic ring)

Rnd 1: Ch 1 (does not count as a st), 8 hdc in ring; join = 8 sts

Fasten off, leaving a long tail for sewing.

Beak

Make 1. Work in rows with **CC4**.

To beg: Ch 2

Row 1: (WS) 3 sc in second ch from hook (the skipped ch does not count as a st); turn = 3 sts

Row 2: (RS) Ch 1 (does not count as a st now and throughout), 2 sc in first st, 3 sc in next st, 2 sc in last st; turn = 7 sts

Row 3: (WS) Ch 1, 2 sc in first st, sc in next 2 sts, 3 sc in next st, sc in next 2 sts, 2 sc in last st; turn = 11 sts

Row 4: (RS) Ch 1, 2 sc in first st, sc in next 4 sts, 3 sc in next st, sc in next 4 sts, 2 sc in last st; do not turn = 15 sts

Row 5: (RS) Ch 1, skip first st, rsc in next 13 sts, sl st in last st = 14 sts

Fasten off, leaving a long tail for sewing.

Face

Make 2 circles and sew them together to finish 1 face. Work in spiral rounds with **CC2**, using a stitch **Marker** to mark the start of each round.

To beg: Ch 3, sl st in third ch from hook to form a ring (or start with a magic ring)

Rnd 1: Ch 1 (does not count as a st), 6 sc in ring; do not join now and throughout = 6 sts

Rnd 2: 2 sc in first st of previous rnd, 2 sc in each of next 5 sts = 12 sts

Rnd 3: 2 sc in each st around = 24 sts

Rnd 4: Sc in each st around = 24 sts

Rnd 5: [Sc in next st, 2 sc in next st] 12 times = 36 sts

Rnd 6: Sc in each st around = 36 sts

Rnd 7: [Sc in next 2 sts, 2 sc in next st] 12 times = 48 sts

Rnd 8: Sc in each st around = 48 sts

Sl st in next st and fasten off, leaving a long tail for sewing. Once both circles are finished, place them side by side and whipstitch across 5 sts using the long tail from one of the circles (fig 2). Fasten off and weave in the end, but keep the tail from the other circle.

Bow

Optional – Make 1. Same as Bow in Lion Block using **CC3**.

Beak

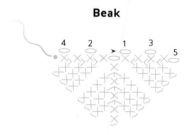

Eye

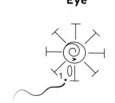

Face

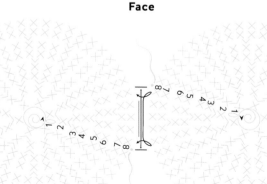

Finishing Block

Depending on the joining method and your project, you can finish the face before or after joining blocks (see Joining Blocks).

To finish the face, sew the eyes in the center of each circle by backstitching around the edge of the eyes using **CC1** tails (fig 2); finish off and weave in the ends. Position the face on the block, 2 rows above the bottom edge of the head, aligning the center of the face with the **Marker**. Backstitch around the face onto the block using **CC2** tails (fig 3). Finish off and weave in the end.

Position the beak in the center of the face, 2 rows above the **Marker**. Using **CC4** tail from the beak, whipstitch across the top edge onto the face and backstitch around the remaining edges (fig 4). Finish off and weave in the end; remove the marker.

Add 2 tassels on the top of the head (see Finishing Touches) or omit tassels if your project will be used by small children.

Optional — Position the bow on the head or under the beak and backstitch around the center onto the block using the long **CC3** tail from the bow. Leave the sides unstitched (figs 4 and 5). Finish off and weave in the end.

Koala Block

Cute and cuddly as can be, koalas enjoy their long sleeps hugging a tree. Since sleeping is a good strategy for conserving energy, a soft koala pillow and a matching blanket will help you get your zzzz's.

MATERIALS

To make this block, use your favorite medium weight acrylic yarn (weight 4) and a 5mm (H) hook or any hook size needed to obtain the gauge (see Tools and Materials). Use the table below to determine the amount required of each color yarn.

GAUGE

14 dc x 8.5 rows = 4 x 4in (10 x 10cm)

FINISHED MEASUREMENTS

Block without border: 12 x 15in (30.5 x 38cm)
Block with border: 15 x 18in (38 x 45.5cm)

Tip

Make adorable sleepy koalas for a pillow, or if you are making a blanket you could use the round eyes from the Pig Block to finish some of the blocks with wide awake koalas.

Chart color	Color key	Color name	Yarn required for 1 block	Yarn required for 4 blocks	Yarn required for 9 blocks	Yarn required for 16 blocks
⬤	MC	Soft White or Baby Yellow	180yd (165m)	720yd (658m)	1620yd (1481m)	2880yd (2633m)
⬤	CC1	Light Gray	80yd (73m)	320yd (293m)	720yd (658m)	1280yd (1170m)
⬤	CC2	Baby Pink	30yd (27m)	120yd (110m)	270yd (247m)	480yd (439m)
⬤	CC3	Black	10yd (9m)	40yd (37m)	90yd (82m)	160yd (146m)

Block

Work in rows using the Intarsia colorwork technique (see Special Stitches). For the background, use **MC** from a skein and wind 1 butterfly-bobbin. For the koala head, use **CC1** from a skein.

To beg: With **MC** from skein – ch 45

Row 1: (RS) Dc in fourth ch from hook (the skipped chs count as dc), dc in each ch across; turn = 43 sts

Rows 2 – 6: Ch 2 (counts as dc now and throughout), skip first st, dc in each st across; turn = 43 sts

With RS facing, place **Marker** in the center stitch of the row just made to indicate the bottom edge of the head. Continue to work in rows, changing colors through the final stage of a stitch before new color indication.

Row 7: (RS) With **MC** from skein – ch 2, skip first st, dc in next 3 sts, dc2tog changing to **CC1** from skein; with **CC1** – 2 dc in next st, dc in next 29 sts, 2 dc in next st changing to **MC** from butterfly-bobbin; with **MC** – dc2tog, dc in next 4 sts; turn = 43 sts

Row 8: (WS) With **MC** – ch 2, skip first st, dc in next 2 sts, dc2tog changing to **CC1**; with **CC1** – 2 dc in next st, dc in next 31 sts, 2 dc in next st changing to **MC**; with **MC** – dc2tog, dc in next 3 sts; turn = 43 sts

Rows 9 – 18: With **MC** – ch 2, skip first st, dc in next 3 sts changing to **CC1**; with **CC1** – dc in next 35 sts changing to **MC**; with **MC** – dc in next 4 sts; turn = 43 sts

Rows 19 – 26: With **MC** – ch 2, skip first st, dc in each st until 1 st left before color change, 2 dc in next st changing to **CC1**; with **CC1** – dc2tog, dc in each st until 2 sts left before color change, dc2tog changing to **MC**; with **MC** – 2 dc in next st, dc in each st to the end; turn = 43 sts

Break off **CC1** and **MC** from the butterfly-bobbin, and use **MC** from the skein for the rest of the block.

Rows 27 – 32: With **MC** – ch 2, skip first st, dc in each st across; turn = 43 sts

Do not fasten off, work 3 rnds of Granny Square Border with **MC** (see Penguin Block).

Cheeks

Make 2. Work in the round with **CC2**.

To beg: Ch 3, sl st in third ch from hook to form a ring (or start with a magic ring)

Rnd 1: Ch 2 (does not count as a st), 12 dc in ring; join = 12 sts

Rnd 2: Ch 1, 2 sc in same st as join, 2 sc in each of next 11 sts; join = 24 sts

Fasten off, leaving a long tail for sewing.

Nose

Make 1. Work in the round with **CC3**.

To beg: Ch 10

Rnd 1: Dc in third ch from hook (the skipped chs do not count as a st), dc in next 6 chs, 6 dc in last ch; work across the opposite side of the foundation ch – dc in next 6 chs, 5 dc in last ch; join = 24 sts

Rnd 2: Ch 1 (does not count as a st), 2 sc in same st as join, sc in next 6 sts, [sc in next st, 2 sc in next st] 3 times, sc in next 7 sts, [2 sc in next st, sc in next st] 2 times; join = 30 sts

Fasten off, leaving a long tail for sewing.

Nose

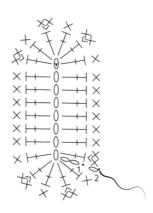

Cheek

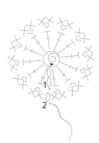

Block

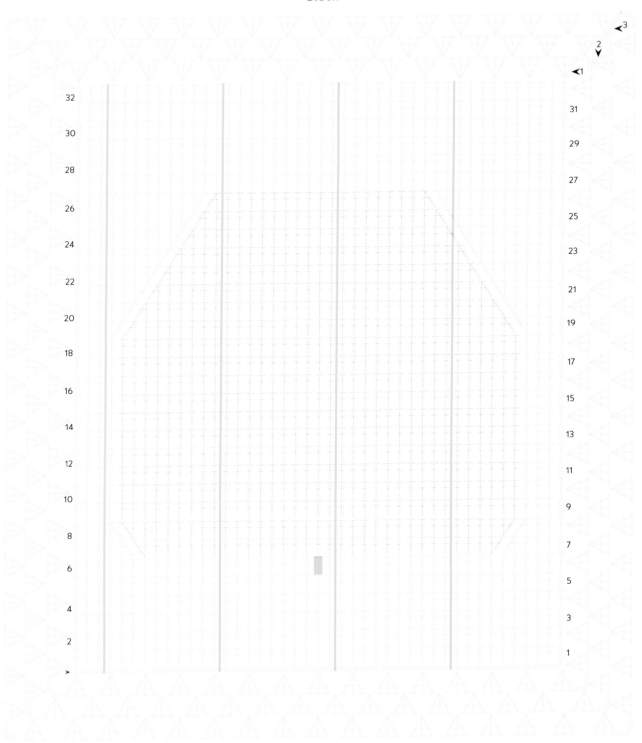

Place **Marker**	—— 10 sts dividers

Ears

Make 2. Work in rows starting with **CC2**.

To beg: With **CC2** – ch 3, sl st in third ch from hook to form a ring (or start with a magic ring)

Row 1: (WS) Ch 2 (counts as dc now and throughout), 6 dc in ring; turn = 7 sts

Row 2: (RS) Ch 2, dc in first st, 2 dc in each of next 5 sts, dc in last st; turn = 13 sts

Row 3: (WS) Ch 2, skip first st, [2 fpdc in next st, bpdc in next st] 5 times, 2 fpdc in next st, dc in last st changing to **CC1**; break off **CC2** leaving a long tail for sewing and turn = 19 sts

Row 4: (RS) With **CC1** – ch 1 (does not count as a st), sc in first st, picot, [sc in next st, picot] 17 times, sl st in last st = 19 sts and 18 picots

Fasten off and weave in **CC1** tails.

Ear

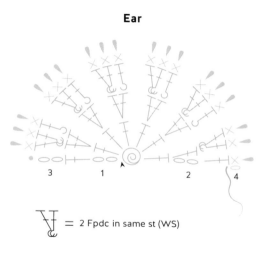

3   1   2   4

V = 2 Fpdc in same st (WS)

Finishing Block

Depending on the joining method and your project, you can finish the face before or after joining blocks (see Joining Blocks).

Position the nose vertically on the head, 3 rows above the center **Marker**. Using the long **CC3** tail from the nose, backstitch around onto the block (fig 1). Finish off and weave in the end.

Position the cheeks on each side of the head, just above the row with **Marker**. Using the long **CC2** tail from each cheek, backstitch around onto the block (fig 1). Finish off, weave in the ends and remove the marker.

Position the ears on each side of the head, with 17 center sts between the ears. Using the long **CC2** tail from each ear, whipstitch across the straight edge onto the block and backstitch around the curved edge just below the picot row (fig 1). Finish off and weave in the ends.

For sleepy eyes, mark 7 sts on each side between the nose and head edge, 3 rows above the cheeks (fig 2). Using **CC3**, make a slipknot and keep the loop on the hook. Insert the hook around the post of the st with first **Marker**, yo and complete fpsc as normal. Work fpsc around the post of the remaining 6 sts (fig 3); fasten off. Finish the second eye in the same manner, weave in the ends and remove the markers.

You can also use round eyes from the Pig Block for some of your Koala Blocks. Position the round eyes on each side between the nose and the head edge, 3 rows above the cheeks. Using the long **CC3** tail from each eye, backstitch around onto the block (fig 4). Finish off and weave in the ends.

Add 3 tassels on the top of the head (see Finishing Touches) and trim the ends. For safety, omit tassels if your project will be used by small children.

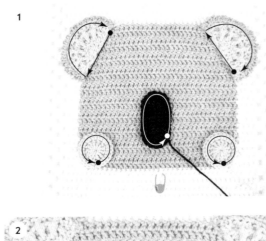

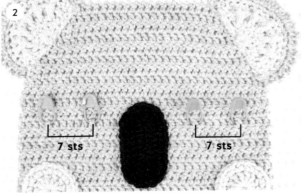

7 sts   7 sts

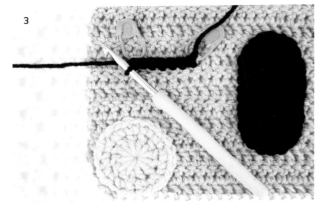

Dog Block

· · · · · · · · · · ·

Your canine friend will love nothing more than to snuggle up with you in a warm doggy blanket. You can make these blocks using the suggested colors or choose your own to replicate your dog.

MATERIALS

To make this block, use your favorite medium weight acrylic yarn (weight 4) and a 5mm (H) hook or any hook size needed to obtain the gauge (see Tools and Materials). Use the table below to determine the amount required of each color yarn.

GAUGE

14 dc x 8.5 rows = 4 x 4in (10 x 10cm)

FINISHED MEASUREMENTS

Block without border: 12 x 15in (30.5 x 38cm)
Block with border: 15 x 18in (38 x 45.5cm)

Tip

· · · · · · · · · · ·

For a more authentic granny square look, or to use up some of your yarn scraps, you could change color in every round of the border.

Chart color	Color key	Color name	Yarn required for 1 block	Yarn required for 4 blocks	Yarn required for 9 blocks	Yarn required for 16 blocks
●	MC	Country Blue or Redwood	180yd (165m)	720yd (658m)	1620yd (1481m)	2880yd (2633m)
●	CC1	Topaz or Black	70yd (64m)	280yd (256m)	630yd (576m)	1120yd (1024m)
●	CC2	Coffee or White	35yd (32m)	140yd (128m)	315yd (288m)	560yd (512m)
●	CC3	Buff or Aran	15yd (14m)	60yd (55m)	135yd (123m)	240yd (220m)
●	CC4	White	5yd (4.5m)	20yd (18m)	45yd (41m)	80yd (73m)
●	CC5	Black	5yd (4.5m)	20yd (18m)	45yd (41m)	80yd (73m)

Block

Work in rows using the Intarsia colorwork technique (see Special Stitches). For the background, use **MC** from a skein and wind 1 butterfly-bobbin. For the dog head, use **CC1** from a skein.

To beg: With **MC** from skein – ch 45

Row 1: (RS) Dc in fourth ch from hook (the skipped chs count as dc), dc in each ch across; turn = 43 sts

Rows 2 – 8: Ch 2 (counts as dc now and throughout), skip first st, dc in each st across; turn = 43 sts

With RS facing, place **Marker** in the center stitch of the row just made to indicate the bottom edge of the head. Continue to work in rows, changing colors through the final stage of a stitch before new color indication.

Row 9: (RS) With **MC** from skein – ch 2, skip first st, dc in next 5 sts, dc2tog changing to **CC1** from skein; with **CC1** – 2 dc in next st, dc in next 25 sts, 2 dc in next st changing to **MC** from butterfly-bobbin; with **MC** – dc2tog, dc in next 6 sts; turn = 43 sts

Rows 10 – 12: With **MC** – ch 2, skip first st, dc in each st until 2 sts left before color change, dc2tog changing to **CC1**; with **CC1** – 2 dc in next st, dc in each st until 1 st left before color change, 2 dc in next st changing to **MC**; with **MC** – dc2tog, dc in each st to the end; turn = 43 sts

Rows 13 – 22: With **MC** – ch 2, skip first st, dc in next 3 sts changing to **CC1**; with **CC1** – dc in next 35 sts changing to **MC**; with **MC** – dc in next 4 sts; turn = 43 sts

Rows 23 – 26: With **MC** – ch 2, skip first st, dc in each st until 1 st left before color change, 2 dc in next st changing to **CC1**; with **CC1** – dc2tog, dc in each st until 2 sts left before color change, dc2tog changing to **MC**; with **MC** – 2 dc in next st, dc in each st to the end; turn = 43 sts

Break off **CC1** and **MC** from the butterfly-bobbin, and use **MC** from the skein for the rest of the block.

Rows 27 – 32: With **MC** – ch 2, skip first st, dc in each st across; turn = 43 sts

Do not fasten off, work 3 rnds of Granny Square Border with **MC** (see Penguin Block).

Muzzle

Make 1. Work in the round with **CC2**.

To beg: Ch 3, sl st in third ch from hook to form a ring (or start with a magic ring)

Rnd 1: Ch 1 (does not count as a st now and throughout), 6 sc in ring; join = 6 sts

Rnd 2: Ch 1, sc in same st as join, 3 sc in next st; [sc in next st, 3 sc in next st] 2 times; join = 12 sts

Rnd 3: Ch 1, sc in same st as join, sc in next st, 3 sc in next st; [sc in next 3 sts, 3 sc in next st] 2 times; sc in next st; join = 18 sts

Rnd 4: Ch 1, sc in same st as join, sc in next 2 sts, 3 sc in next st; [sc in next 5 sts, 3 sc in next st] 2 times; sc in next 2 sts; join = 24 sts

Rnd 5: Ch 1, sc in same st as join, sc in next 3 sts, 3 sc in next st; [sc in next 7 sts, 3 sc in next st] 2 times; sc in next 3 sts; join = 30 sts

Rnd 6: Ch 1, sc in same st as join, sc in next 4 sts, 3 sc in next st; [sc in next 9 sts, 3 sc in next st] 2 times; sc in next 4 sts; join = 36 sts

Rnd 7: Ch 1, sc in same st as join, sc in next 5 sts, 3 sc in next st, sc in next 10 sts, 2 sc in next st, sc in next st and place **Marker** in st just made, 2 sc in next st, sc in next 10 sts, 3 sc in next st, sc in next 5 sts; join = 42 sts

Fasten off, leaving a long tail for sewing.

Muzzle

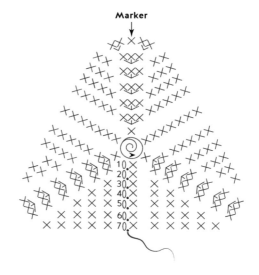

Block

⊤ Place **Marker**   ——— 10 sts dividers

Eyes

Make 2 outer eyes with **CC4** and 2 pupils with **CC5** to complete 2 eyes. Work in the round.

OUTER EYES

To beg: Ch 3, sl st in third ch from hook to form a ring (or start with a magic ring)

Rnd 1: Ch 2 (does not count as a st), 12 dc in ring; join = 12 sts

Fasten off, leaving a long tail for sewing.

PUPILS

To beg: Ch 3, sl st in third ch from hook to form a ring (or start with a magic ring)

Rnd 1: Ch 1 (does not count as a st), 6 sc in ring; join = 6 sts

Fasten off, leaving a long tail for sewing.

FINISHING EYES

Thread the needle with **CC4** and stitch a highlight on each pupil; finish off and weave in the ends. Position the pupil in the center of the outer eye and backstitch around using **CC5** tail from the pupil (fig 1); finish off and weave in the end. Complete the second eye in the same manner.

Nose

Make 1. Same as Nose in Panda Block using **CC5**.

Ears

Make 2. Work in rows with **CC2**.

To beg: Ch 7

Row 1: (WS) Sc in second ch from hook (the skipped ch does not count as a st), sc in next 4 chs, 3 sc in last ch and place **Marker** in the center st of 3-sc group just made; work across the opposite side of the foundation ch – sc in next 5 chs; turn = 13 sts

Rows 2 – 6: Ch 1 (does not count as a st), sc in first st, sc in each st to **Marker**, 3 sc in marked st and move **Marker** to the center st of 3-sc group, sc in each st to the end; turn = 23 sts after the last row

Fasten off, leaving a long tail for sewing and remove the marker.

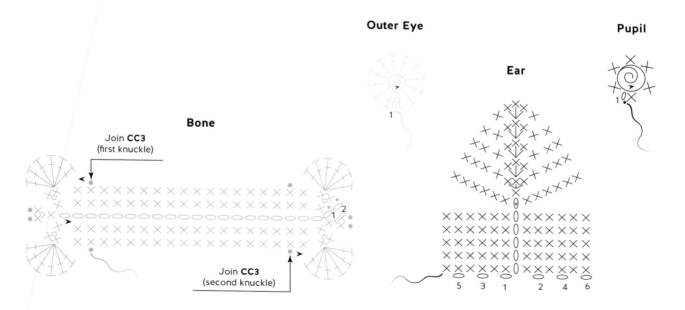

Outer Eye

Pupil

Ear

Bone

Join **CC3**
(first knuckle)

Join **CC3**
(second knuckle)

5 3 1 2 4 6

Bone

Optional – Make 1. Work in the round with **CC3**.

To beg: Ch 21

Rnd 1: Sc in second ch from hook (the skipped ch does not count as a st), sc in next 18 chs, 3 sc in last ch; work across the opposite side of the foundation ch – sc in next 18 chs, 2 sc in last ch; join = 42 sts

Rnd 2: Ch 1 (does not count as a st), 2 sc in same st as join, sc in next 18 sts, 2 sc in each of next 3 sts, sc in next 18 sts, 2 sc in each of next 2 sts; join = 48 sts

Fasten off and weave in the ends. Mark 10 sts on each end of the finished shape (fig 2) and work each knuckle as follows:

KNUCKLE: Join **CC3** in st with first **Marker**, skip next st, 6 dc in next st, skip st, sl st in next 2 sts, skip st, 6 dc in next st, skip st, sl st in last st with **Marker**; remove both markers.

Fasten off, leaving a long tail for sewing. Finish the second knuckle in the same manner and weave in the ends.

Finishing Block

Depending on the joining method and your project, you can finish the face before or after joining blocks (see Joining Blocks).

Position the muzzle on the head with its **Marker** facing upwards, centering the bottom edge of the muzzle right above the **Marker** on the block. Using **CC2** tail from the muzzle, backstitch around onto the block (fig 3). Finish off and weave in the end.

Position the nose below the top **Marker** on the muzzle and backstitch around onto the muzzle using **CC5** tail from the nose (fig 4). Finish off, weave in the end and remove the markers.

Position the eyes on each side of the muzzle, 3 - 4 sts away from the head edges. Backstitch around each eye onto the block with **CC4** tails (fig 4). Finish off and weave in the ends.

Position the ears on each side of the head, with the raw edges around the curves and pin them in place. Using **CC2** tails, whipstitch across the bottom edge of each ear onto the block, leaving the remaining edges unstitched (fig 4). Finish off, weave in the ends and fold the ears down towards the face.

Optional – Position the bone below the head and backstitch around onto the block using the long **CC3** tail. Finish off and weave in the end.

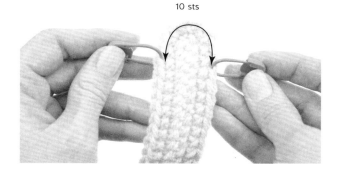

10 sts

Panda Block

Snuggle up in your chair while making a classy panda blanket for your little rock star. You can use the same background color for all your blocks or alternate dark and light shades for a checkerboard look.

MATERIALS

To make this block, use your favorite medium weight acrylic yarn (weight 4) and a 5mm (H) hook or any hook size needed to obtain the gauge (see Tools and Materials). Use the table below to determine the amount required of each color yarn.

GAUGE

14 dc x 8.5 rows = 4 x 4in (10 x 10cm)

FINISHED MEASUREMENTS

Block without border: 12 x 15in (30.5 x 38cm)
Block with border: 15 x 18in (38 x 45.5cm)

Tip

Opt for different shaped eye patches, and you could also alternate the position of the star patch, to mix up the look of your Panda Blocks.

Chart color	Color key	Color name	Yarn required for 1 block	Yarn required for 4 blocks	Yarn required for 9 blocks	Yarn required for 16 blocks
●	MC	Aqua or Teal Heather	180yd (165m)	720yd (658m)	1620yd (1481m)	2880yd (2633m)
●	CC1	White	90yd (82m)	360yd (330m)	810yd (741m)	1440yd (1317m)
●	CC2	Black	40yd (37m)	160yd (146m)	360yd (330m)	640yd (585m)
●	CC3	Baby Pink	10yd (9m)	40yd (37m)	90yd (82m)	160yd (146m)

Block

Work in rows using the Intarsia colorwork technique (see Special Stitches). For the background, use **MC** from a skein and wind 1 butterfly-bobbin. For the panda head, use **CC1** from a skein.

To beg: With **MC** from skein – ch 45

Row 1: (RS) Dc in fourth ch from hook (the skipped chs count as dc), dc in each ch across; turn = 43 sts

Rows 2 – 6: Ch 2 (counts as dc now and throughout), skip first st, dc in each st across; turn = 43 sts

With RS facing, place **Marker** in the center stitch of the row just made to indicate the bottom edge of the head. Continue to work in rows, changing colors through the final stage of a stitch before new color indication.

Row 7: (RS) With **MC** from skein – ch 2, skip first st, dc in next 5 sts, dc2tog changing to **CC1** from skein; with **CC1** – 2 dc in next st, dc in next 25 sts, 2 dc in next st changing to **MC** from butterfly-bobbin; with **MC** – dc2tog, dc in next 6 sts; turn = 43 sts

Rows 8 – 10: With **MC** – ch 2, skip first st, dc in each st until 2 sts left before color change, dc2tog changing to **CC1**; with **CC1** – 2 dc in next st, dc in each st until 1 st left before color change, 2 dc in next st changing to **MC**; with **MC** – dc2tog, dc in each st to the end; turn = 43 sts

Rows 11 – 22: With **MC** – ch 2, skip first st, dc in next 3 sts changing to **CC1**; with **CC1** – dc in next 35 sts changing to **MC**; with **MC** – dc in next 4 sts; turn = 43 sts

Rows 23 – 26: With **MC** – ch 2, skip first st, dc in each st until 1 st left before color change, 2 dc in next st changing to **CC1**; with **CC1** – dc2tog, dc in each st until 2 sts left before color change, dc2tog changing to **MC**; with **MC** – 2 dc in next st, dc in each st to the end; turn = 43 sts

Break off **CC1** and **MC** from the butterfly-bobbin, and use **MC** from the skein for the rest of the block.

Rows 27 – 32: With **MC** – ch 2, skip first st, dc in each st across; turn = 43 sts

Do not fasten off, work 3 rnds of Granny Square Border with **MC** (see Penguin Block).

Eyes

Make 2. Same as Eyes in Dog Block but omit highlights. Use **CC1** for the outer eyes and **CC2** for pupils.

Eye Patches

Make 1 oval patch and 1 star patch or 2 oval patches. Work in the round with **CC2**.

OVAL PATCH

To beg: Ch 9

Rnd 1: Dc in third ch from hook (the skipped chs do not count as a st), dc in next 5 chs, 6 dc in last ch; work across the opposite side of the foundation ch – dc in next 5 chs, 5 dc in last ch; join = 22 sts

Rnd 2: Ch 1 (does not count as a st), 2 sc in same st as join, hdc in next 5 sts, 2 dc in each of next 6 sts, hdc in next 5 sts, [sc in next st, 2 sc in next st] 2 times, sc in last st; join = 31 sts

Fasten off, leaving a long tail for sewing.

Oval Patch

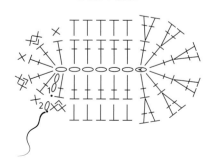

Block

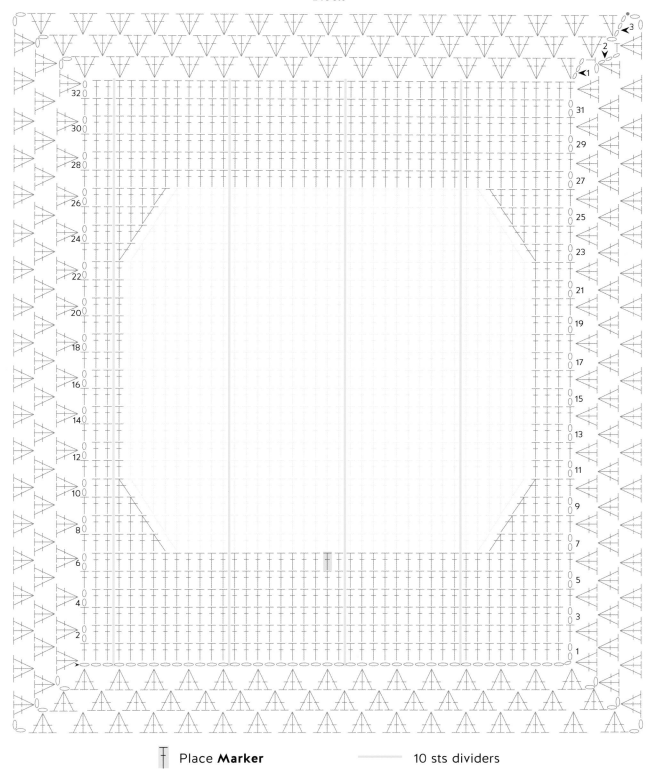

 Place **Marker**   ───── 10 sts dividers

STAR PATCH

To beg: Ch 3, sl st in third ch from hook to form a ring (or start with a magic ring)

Rnd 1: Ch 2 (does not count as a st), 10 dc in ring; join = 10 sts

Rnd 2: Ch 1 (does not count as a st), 2 sc in same st as join, 2 sc in each of next 9 sts; join = 20 sts

Rnd 3: Skip st with join, [ch 7, sc in second ch from hook, hdc in next ch, dc in next 2 chs, tr in final 2 chs, skip 3 sts, sl st in next st] 5 times = 5 star points

Fasten off, leaving a long tail for sewing.

FINISHING PATCHES

Position the eye by the narrow end of an oval patch or in the middle of a star patch. Using the long **CC1** tail from each eye, backstitch around onto the patch (fig 1). Finish off and weave in the ends.

Cheeks

Optional — Make 2. Work in the round with **CC3**.

To beg: Ch 3, sl st in third ch from hook to form a ring (or start with a magic ring)

Rnd 1: Ch 2 (does not count as a st), 10 dc in ring; join = 10 sts

Rnd 2: Ch 1 (does not count as a st), 2 sc in same st as join, 2 sc in each of next 9 sts; join = 20 sts

Fasten off, leaving a long tail for sewing.

Nose

Make 1. Work in the round with **CC2**.

To beg: Ch 5

Rnd 1: Hdc in second ch from hook (the skipped ch does not count as a st), hdc in next 2 chs, 4 hdc in last ch; work across the opposite side of the foundation ch – hdc in next 2 chs, 3 hdc in last ch; join = 12 sts

Fasten off, leaving a long tail for sewing.

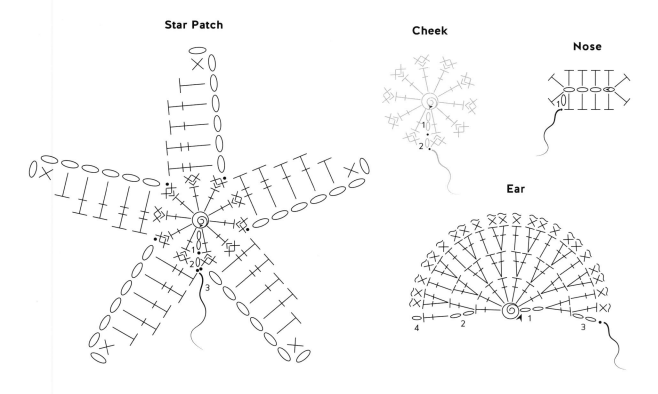

Star Patch

Cheek

Nose

Ear

Ears

Make 2. Work in rows with **CC2**.

To beg: Ch 3, sl st in third ch from hook to form a ring (or start with a magic ring)

Row 1: (RS) Ch 2 (counts as dc now and throughout), 7 dc in ring; turn = 8 sts

Row 2: (WS) Ch 2, dc in first st, 2 dc in each of next 7 sts; turn = 16 sts

Row 3: (RS) Ch 2, dc in first st, [dc in next st, 2 dc in next st] 7 times, dc in last st; do not turn = 24 sts

Row 4: (RS) Ch 1 (does not count as a st), skip first st, rsc in next 22 sts, sl st in last st = 23 sts

Fasten off, leaving a long tail for sewing.

Finishing Block

Depending on the joining method and your project, you can finish the face before or after joining blocks (see Joining Blocks).

Position the nose horizontally on the head, 5 rows above the center **Marker**. Using the long **CC2** tail from the nose, backstitch around onto the block, then chain stitch 2 rows down from the center of the nose (fig 2). Finish off, weave in the end and remove the marker.

Optional – Position the cheeks on each side of the head, just above the bottom edge. Using the long **CC3** tail from each cheek, backstitch around onto the block (fig 3). Finish off and weave in the ends.

Position the oval patches at a 45 degree angle on each side of the nose, placing them right up against the head edges (fig 3). You can replace one of the oval patches with a star patch (fig 2). Using the long **CC2** tail from each patch, backstitch around the edge onto the block. Finish off and weave in the ends.

Position the ears on each side of the head, with the raw edges around the curves and pin them in place. Using the long **CC2** tail from each ear, whipstitch across the bottom edge onto the block and backstitch around the outer edge of the ears (fig 4). Finish off and weave in the ends.

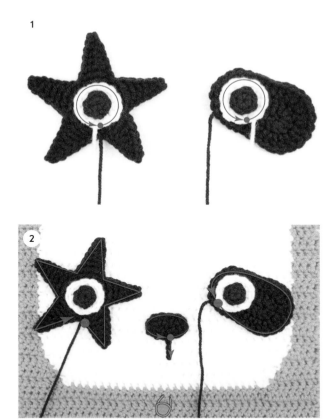

Pig Block

After running around and playing, your little critters will appreciate an afternoon nap on a soft piggy pillow with a cute blanket. A matching toy bag can also make clean up time much easier.

MATERIALS

To make this block, use your favorite medium weight acrylic yarn (weight 4) and a 5mm (H) hook or any hook size needed to obtain the gauge (see Tools and Materials). Use the table below to determine the amount required of each color yarn.

GAUGE

14 dc x 8.5 rows = 4 x 4in (10 x 10cm)

FINISHED MEASUREMENTS

Block without border: 12 x 15in (30.5 x 38cm)
Block with border: 15 x 18in (38 x 45.5cm)

Tip

Make a big bow to go under the snout, or a smaller bow to sew onto the head below the ear. Either way, it's a very cute addition to your Pig Block.

Chart color	Color key	Color name	Yarn required for 1 block	Yarn required for 4 blocks	Yarn required for 9 blocks	Yarn required for 16 blocks
●	MC	Coffee or Redwood	180yd (165m)	720yd (658m)	1620yd (1481m)	2880yd (2633m)
●	CC1	Petal Pink or Baby Pink	120yd (110m)	480yd (439m)	1080yd (988m)	1920yd (1756m)
●	CC2	Soft Rose or Perfect Pink	12yd (11m)	48yd (44m)	108yd (99m)	192yd (176m)
●	CC3	Carrot or Redwood	15–30yd (14–27m)	60–120yd (55–110m)	135–270yd (123–247m)	240–480yd (220–439m)
●	CC4	Black	3yd (3m)	12yd (11m)	27yd (25m)	48yd (44m)
○	CC5	White	1yd (1m)	4yd (4m)	9yd (8.5m)	16yd (15m)

Block

Same as Panda Block using **MC** and **CC1**.

Snout

Make 1. Work in the round with **CC2**.

To beg: Ch 3, sl st in third ch from hook to form a ring (or start with a magic ring)

Rnd 1: Ch 1 (does not count as a st now and throughout), 6 sc in ring; join = 6 sts

Rnd 2: Ch 1, sc in same st as join, 3 sc in next st, [sc in next st, 3 sc in next st] 2 times; join = 12 sts

Rnd 3: Ch 1, sc in same st as join, sc in next st, 3 sc in next st, [sc in next 3 sts, 3 sc in next st] 2 times, sc in next st; join = 18 sts

Rnd 4: Ch 1, sc in same st as join, sc in next 2 sts, 3 sc in next st, [sc in next 5 sts, 3 sc in next st] 2 times, sc in next 2 sts; join = 24 sts

Rnd 5: Ch 1, sc in same st as join, sc in next 3 sts, 3 sc in next st, [sc in next 7 sts, 3 sc in next st] 2 times, sc in next 3 sts; join = 30 sts

Rnd 6: Ch 1, sc in same st as join, sc in next 4 sts, 3 sc in next st, sc in next 9 sts, 3 sc in next st, place **Marker** in the center st of 3-sc group just made, sc in next 9 sts, 3 sc in next st, sc in next 4 sts; join = 36 sts

Fasten off, leaving a long tail for sewing.

Ears

Make 2. Work in the round with **CC1**.

To beg: Ch 3, sl st in third ch from hook to form a ring (or start with a magic ring)

Rnds 1 – 6: Same as for Snout but omit marker

Rnd 7: Ch 1, sc in same st as join, sc in next 5 sts, 3 sc in next st, [sc in next 11 sts, 3 sc in next st] 2 times, sc in next 5 sts; join = 42 sts

Fasten off, leaving a long tail for sewing.

Eyes

Make 2. Work in the round with **CC4**.

To beg: Ch 3, sl st in third ch from hook to form a ring (or start with a magic ring)

Rnd 1: Ch 1 (does not count as a st), 8 hdc in ring; join = 8 sts

Fasten off, leaving a long tail for sewing. Thread the needle with **CC5** and stitch a highlight on each eye.

Bow

Optional – Make 1 small bow as for Lion Block or 1 big bow as for Monkey Block. Work with **CC3**.

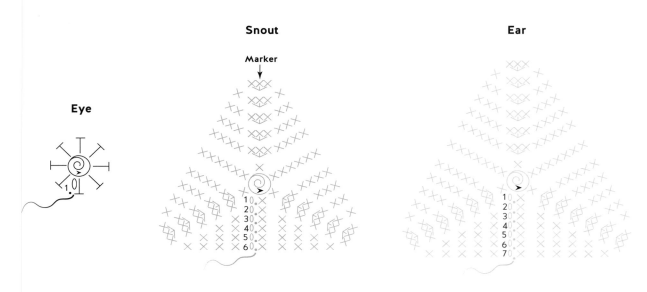

Eye

Snout

Marker

Ear

Finishing Block

Depending on the joining method and your project, you can finish the face before or after joining blocks (see Joining Blocks).

Position the snout on the head with its **Marker** facing upwards, centering the bottom edge of the snout right above the **Marker** on the block. Using the long **CC2** tail from the snout, backstitch around onto the block (fig 1). Thread the needle with **CC1** and stitch nostrils on each side of the muzzle (fig 2). Finish off, weave in the ends and remove the markers.

Position the ears at a 45 degree angle on each side of the head, with 13 center sts between the ears. With **CC1** tail from each ear, backstitch across the bottom edge onto the block, then backstitch to the center of the ear, down to the next bottom corner and back to the starting point. Leave the side edges unstitched (fig 3). Finish off and weave in the ends.

Position the eyes on each side between the snout and the head edge, just above the snout. Using the long **CC4** tail from each eye, backstitch around onto the block (fig 4). Finish off and weave in the ends.

Big Bow (optional) – Position the bow under the snout and whipstitch across the top and bottom edges onto the block with **CC3** tails, leaving the sides unstitched. Finish off and weave in the ends.

Small Bow (optional) – Position the bow on the head and backstitch around the center onto the block with **CC3** tail, leaving the sides unstitched. Finish off and weave in the end.

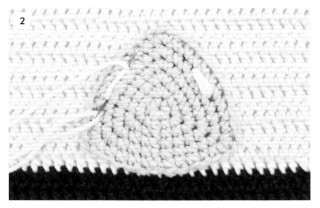

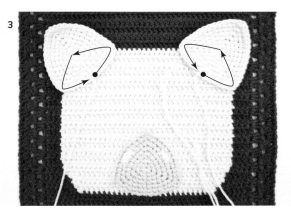

Monkey Block

Your kids will go bananas over a cheeky monkey blanket with matching accessories. You can add a bow on the top of the monkey's head, under the chin, or mix blocks with different bow accents.

MATERIALS

To make this block, use your favorite medium weight acrylic yarn (weight 4) and a 5mm (H) hook or any hook size needed to obtain the gauge (see Tools and Materials). Use the table below to determine the amount required of each color yarn.

GAUGE

14 dc x 8.5 rows = 4 x 4in (10 x 10cm)

FINISHED MEASUREMENTS

Block without border: 12 x 15in (30.5 x 38cm)
Block with border: 15 x 18in (38 x 45.5cm)

Tip

Use colorful yarn scraps to make different bows and add a splash of rainbow onto your blanket. Colorful monkey smiles on a blanket are also a fun idea.

Chart color	Color key	Color name	Yarn required for 1 block	Yarn required for 4 blocks	Yarn required for 9 blocks	Yarn required for 16 blocks
●	MC	Aran	240yd (220m)	960yd (878m)	2160yd (1975m)	3840yd (3511m)
●	CC1	Chocolate Tweed or Coffee	60yd (55m)	240yd (220m)	540yd (494m)	960yd (878m)
●	CC2	Topaz	60yd (55m)	240yd (220m)	540yd (494m)	960yd (878m)
●	CC3	Bright Yellow	30yd (27m)	120yd (110m)	270yd (247m)	480yd (439m)
●	CC4	Hot Red	2yd (2m)	8yd (7m)	18yd (16.5m)	32yd (29m)
●	CC5	Buff	1yd (1m)	4yd (4m)	9yd (8.5m)	16yd (15m)

Block

Work in rows using the Intarsia colorwork technique (see Special Stitches). For the background, use **MC** from a skein and wind 1 butterfly-bobbin. For the monkey head, use **CC1** from a skein.

To beg: With **MC** from skein – ch 45

Row 1: (RS) Dc in fourth ch from hook (the skipped chs count as dc), dc in each ch across; turn = 43 sts

Rows 2 – 14: Ch 2 (counts as dc now and throughout), skip first st, dc in each st across; turn = 43 sts

With RS facing, place **Marker** in the center stitch of the row just made to indicate the bottom edge of the head. Continue to work in rows, changing colors through the final stage of a stitch before new color indication.

Rows 15 – 20: With **MC** from skein – ch 2, skip first st, dc in next 5 sts changing to **CC1** from skein; with **CC1** – dc in next 31 sts changing to **MC** from butterfly-bobbin; with **MC** – dc in next 6 sts; turn = 43 sts

With RS facing, place **Marker** on each side of **CC1** section of the row just made to indicate the ears placement.

Rows 21 – 26: With **MC** – ch 2, skip first st, dc in each st until 1 st left before color change, 2 dc in next st changing to **CC1**; with **CC1** – dc2tog, dc in each st until 2 sts left before color change, dc2tog changing to **MC**; with **MC** – 2 dc in next st, dc in each st to the end; turn = 43 sts

Break off **CC1** and **MC** from the butterfly-bobbin, and use **MC** from the skein for the rest of the block.

Rows 27 – 32: With **MC** – ch 2, skip first st, dc in each st across; turn = 43 sts

Do not fasten off, work 3 rnds of Granny Square Border with **MC** (see Penguin Block).

Ears

Make 2. Same as Ears in Lion Block using **CC1**.

Hair

Make 1. Same as Whiskers in Cat Block using **CC1**.

Muzzle

Make 1. Work in the round with **CC2**.

To beg: Ch 25

Rnd 1: Dc in third ch from hook (the skipped chs do not count as a st), dc in next 21 chs, 6 dc in last ch; work across the opposite side of the foundation ch – dc in next 21 chs, 5 dc in last ch; join = 54 sts

Rnd 2: Ch 2 (does not count as a st now and throughout), 2 dc in same st as join, dc in next 21 sts, 2 dc in each of next 6 sts, dc in next 21 sts, 2 dc in each of next 5 sts; join = 66 sts

Rnd 3: Ch 2, dc in same st as join, 2 dc in next st, dc in next 21 sts, [dc in next st, 2 dc in next st] 6 times, dc in next 21 sts, [dc in next st, 2 dc in next st] 5 times; join = 78 sts

Rnd 4: Ch 2, 2 dc in same st as join, dc in next 23 sts, [2 dc in next st, dc in next 2 sts] 6 times, dc in next 21 sts, [2 dc in next st, dc in next 2 sts] 5 times; join = 90 sts

Fasten off, leaving a long tail for sewing.

Muzzle

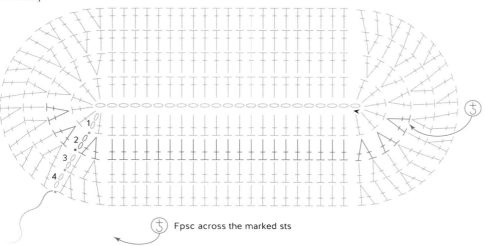

🅢 Fpsc across the marked sts

Block

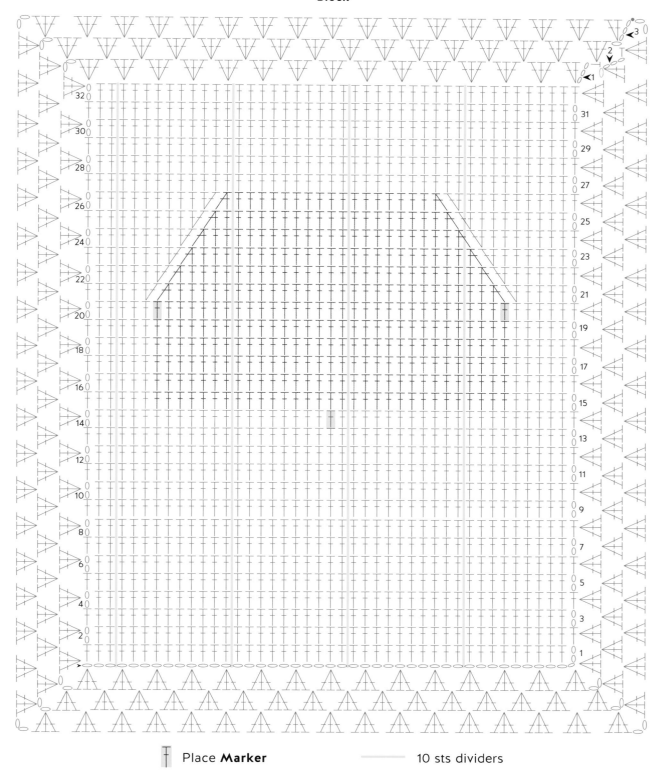

| Place **Marker** | 10 sts dividers |

FINISHING SMILE

With RS facing, mark the bottom half of Rnd 2 for the smile (33 stitches). Work around the marked stitches with **CC4** as follows: Make a slipknot and keep the loop on the hook, insert the hook around the post of the first marked st, yo and complete fpsc as normal. Work fpsc around the post of the remaining 32 sts (fig 1). Fasten off and weave in **CC4** ends.

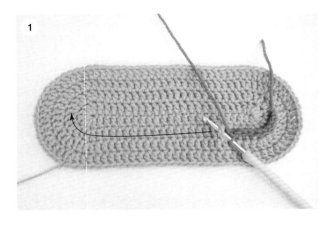

Eye Patches

Make 2. Work in rows with **CC2**.

To beg: Ch 6

Row 1: (RS) Dc in fourth ch from hook (the skipped chs count as dc), dc in next ch, 6 dc in last ch; work across the opposite side of the foundation ch − dc in next 3 chs; turn = 12 sts

Row 2: (WS) Ch 2 (counts as dc now and throughout), skip first st, dc in next 2 sts, 2 dc in each of next 6 sts, dc in final 3 sts; turn = 18 sts

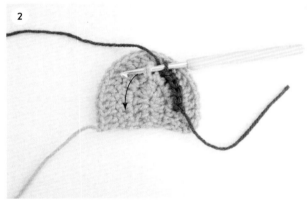

Row 3: (RS) Ch 2, skip first st, dc in next 2 sts, [2 dc in next st, dc in next st] 6 times, dc in final 3 sts = 24 sts

Fasten off, leaving a long tail for sewing.

FINISHING PATCHES

With RS facing, skip 3 sts on each side of Row 2 and mark the middle 12 sts for the eye. Work around the marked stitches with **CC1** as follows: Make a slipknot and keep the loop on the hook, insert the hook around the post of the first marked st, yo and complete fpsc as normal. Work fpsc around the post of the remaining 11 sts (fig 2). Fasten off and weave in **CC1** ends.

Place the 2 patches side by side with the flat edges facing down. Using the long **CC2** tail between the patches, whipstitch across 5 sts to join them. Fasten off and weave in the end; leave the other long tail for later.

Bow

Optional – Make 1. Begin by working in the round with **CC3**.

To beg: Ch 3, sl st in third ch from hook to form a ring (or start with a magic ring)

Rnd 1: Ch 1 (does not count as a st now and throughout), 6 sc in ring; join = 6 sts

Rnd 2: Beg PC in same st as join, ch 2, [PC in next st, ch 2] 5 times; join = 6 PC and 6 ch-2 sps

Rnd 3: Ch 1, [skip PC, 3 sc in next ch-2 sp] 6 times; join = 18 sts

Row 4: (RS) Ch 1, 3 sc in same st as join, 3 sc in each of next 3 sts; *skip 5 sts and place **Marker** in next st**; leaving the remaining sts unworked; turn and continue to work in rows from now on = 12 sts

Rows 5 – 10: Ch 1, sc in first st, sc in each st across; turn = 12 sts

Fasten off, leaving a long tail for sewing. With RS facing, join **CC2** in st with **Marker** and remove the marker. Repeat **Rows 4 – 10**, omitting the instructions from * to **. Fasten off, leaving a long tail for sewing.

Finishing Block

Depending on the joining method and your project, you can finish the face before or after joining blocks (see Joining Blocks).

Position the eye patches with the seam above the center **Marker** on the block. Using the long **CC2** tail, whipstitch across the bottom edge onto the block and backstitch around the curved edges (fig 3). Finish off, weave in the end and remove the center marker.

Position the ears on each side of the head, aligning the center of the ears with the side **Markers**. Using the long **CC1** tail from each ear, whipstitch across the bottom edge onto the block and backstitch around the outer edge of the ears (fig 3). Finish off, weave in the ends and remove the markers.

Position the hair on the top of the head and whipstitch across the bottom edge onto the block using the long **CC1** tail (fig 3). Finish off and weave in the end.

Position the muzzle across the bottom edge of the head, covering the bottom edge of the patches. Using the long **CC2** tail from the muzzle, backstitch around the edge onto the block. Finish off and weave in the end.

To finish nostrils, mark 5 center sts across the top edge of the muzzle and 1 center st of 2 rounds below. Thread the needle with **CC5** and chain stitch the V-shaped nostrils (fig 4). Finish off and weave in the end.

Optional – Position the bow on the top of the head or under the chin and whipstitch across the top and bottom edges using the long **CC3** tail from each side. Finish off and weave in the ends.

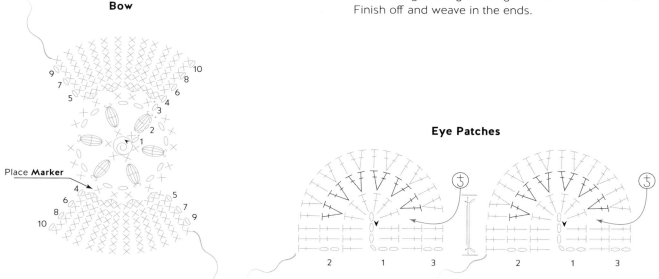

Bow

Place **Marker**

Eye Patches

Hippo Block

· · · · · · · · · · ·

Happy hippo the hippopotamus will be loved a-lot-amus because it's too cute for words! With silly eyes and floppy ears, this hippo is sure to raise a smile!

MATERIALS

To make this block, use your favorite medium weight acrylic yarn (weight 4) and a 5mm (H) hook or any hook size needed to obtain the gauge (see Tools and Materials). Use the table below to determine the amount required of each color yarn.

GAUGE

14 dc x 8.5 rows = 4 x 4in (10 x 10cm)

FINISHED MEASUREMENTS

Block without border: 12 x 15in (30.5 x 38cm)
Block with border: 15 x 18in (38 x 45.5cm)

Tip

· · · · · · · · · · ·

You can alternate aquatic blue backgrounds to highlight the habitat that hippos enjoy. For a modern look, change color placement in every other block by reversing the hippo and background colors.

Chart color	Color key	Color name	Yarn required for 1 block	Yarn required for 4 blocks	Yarn required for 9 blocks	Yarn required for 16 blocks
●	MC	Blue or Light Blue	240yd (220m)	960yd (878m)	2160yd (1975m)	3840yd (3511m)
●	CC1	Light Gray	110yd (101m)	440yd (402m)	990yd (905m)	1760yd (1609m)
●	CC2	White	15yd (14m)	60yd (55m)	135yd (123m)	240yd (220m)
●	CC3	Black	3yd (3m)	12yd (11m)	27yd (25m)	48yd (44m)
●	CC4	Petal Pink	2yd (2m)	8yd (7m)	18yd (16.5m)	32yd (29m)

Block

Same as Monkey Block, but omit markers in Row 20. Work with **MC** and **CC1**.

Muzzle

Make 1. Work in the round with **CC1**.

To beg: Ch 31

Rnd 1: Dc in third ch from hook (the skipped chs do not count as a st), dc in next 27 chs, 6 dc in last ch; work across the opposite side of the foundation ch – dc in next 27 chs, 5 dc in last ch; join = 66 sts

Rnd 2: Ch 2 (does not count as a st now and throughout), dc in same st as join, dc in next 28 sts, 5 dc in next st, dc in next 2 sts, 5 dc in next st, dc in next 29 sts, 5 dc in next st, dc in next 2 sts, 5 dc in next st; join = 82 sts

Rnd 3: Ch 2, dc in same st as join, dc in next 30 sts, 5 dc in next st, dc in next 6 sts, 5 dc in next st, dc in next 33 sts, 5 dc in next st, dc in next 6 sts, 5 dc in next st, dc in next 2 sts; join = 98 sts

Rnd 4: Ch 2, dc in same st as join, dc in next 32 sts, 5 dc in next st, dc in next 10 sts, 5 dc in next st, dc in next 37 sts, 5 dc in next st, dc in next 10 sts, 5 dc in next st, dc in next 4 sts; join = 114 sts

Fasten off, leaving a long tail for sewing.

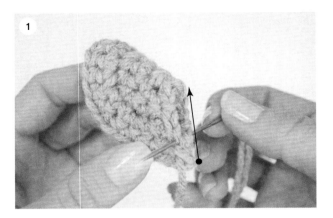

Muzzle

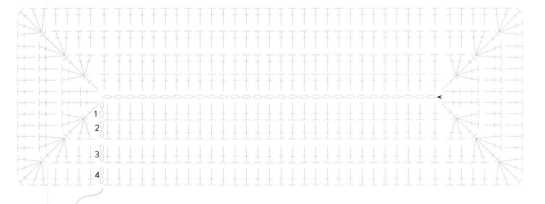

Outer Eye

Ears

Make 2. Work in rows with **CC1**.

To beg: Ch 3, sl st in third ch from hook to form a ring (or start with a magic ring)

Row 1: (RS) Ch 1 (does not count as a st now and throughout), 5 sc in ring; turn = 5 sts

Row 2: (WS) Ch 1, 2 sc in first st, 2 sc in each of next 4 sts; turn = 10 sts

Row 3: (RS) Ch 1, sc in first st, 2 sc in next st, [sc in next st, 2 sc in next st] 4 times; turn = 15 sts

Row 4: (WS) Ch 1, sc in first st, sc in next st, 2 sc in next st, [sc in next 2 sts, 2 sc in next st] 4 times; turn = 20 sts

Row 5: (RS) Ch 1, sc in first st, sc in next 2 sts, 2 sc in next st, [sc in next 3 sts, 2 sc in next st] 4 times = 25 sts

Fasten off, leaving a long tail for sewing. Fold the ear in half and whipstitch across the bottom edge (fig 1). Do not weave in the end yet.

Nostrils

Make 2. Work in the round with **CC4**.

To beg: Ch 3, sl st in third ch from hook to form a ring (or start with a magic ring)

Rnd 1: Ch 1 (does not count as a st), 6 sc in ring; join = 6 sts

Fasten off, leaving a long tail for sewing.

Teeth

Make 2. Work in rows with **CC2**.

To beg: Ch 5

Row 1: Sc in second ch from hook (the skipped ch does not count as a st), sc in next 2 chs, 4 sc in last ch; work across the opposite side of the foundation ch – sc in next 3 chs = 10 sts

Fasten off, leaving a long tail for sewing.

Eyes

Make 2 pupils using **CC3** – same as Eyes in Pig Block and stitch highlights with **CC2**, then make 2 outer eyes using **CC2** as follows:

To beg: Ch 5

Rnd 1: Sc in second ch from hook (the skipped ch does not count as a st), sc in next ch, hdc in next ch, (hdc, 3 dc, hdc) in last ch; work across the opposite side of the foundation ch – hdc in next ch, sc in next ch, 2 sc in last ch; join = 12 sts

Rnd 2: Ch 1 (does not count as a st), 2 sc in same st as join, sc in next 2 sts, 2 sc in each of next 5 sts, sc in next 2 sts, 2 sc in each of next 2 sts; join = 20 sts

Fasten off, leaving a long tail for sewing. Position the pupil by the narrow end of the outer eye and backstitch around using the long **CC3** tail from the pupil. Finish off and weave in the end.

Finishing Block

Depending on the joining method and your project, you can finish the face before or after joining blocks (see Joining Blocks).

Position the nostrils on each side of the muzzle, in the top corners of Rnd 2. Backstitch around onto the muzzle using **CC4** tails. Finish off and weave in the ends.

Position the muzzle to cover the bottom edge of the head, centering it above the **Marker** and remove the marker. Position the teeth on each side under the bottom edge of the muzzle and sew them onto the block using the long **CC2** tail from each tooth – whipstitch across the top edge onto the block and backstitch around the remaining edges (fig 2). Using the long **CC1** tail, backstitch the muzzle around onto the block (fig 3). Finish off and weave in the ends.

Position the ears on each side of the head, with 17 center sts between the ears. Using the long **CC1** tail from each ear, whipstitch across the seamed edge onto the block (fig 3). Finish off and weave in the ends.

Position the eyes in the center of the head above the muzzle and backstitch around onto the block with **CC2** tails (fig 3). Finish off and weave in the ends.

Ear

Tooth

Nostril

Cat Block

· · · · · · · · · · · · ·

Make a purr-fect blanket for your feline fans. You can
alternate the colors of the cat, background and eyes,
or add paws and a bow. The paw-sibilities are endless!

MATERIALS

To make this block, use your favorite medium
weight acrylic yarn (weight 4) and a 5mm (H) hook
or any hook size needed to obtain the gauge
(see Tools and Materials). Use the table below to
determine the amount required of each color yarn.

GAUGE

14 dc x 8.5 rows = 4 x 4in (10 x 10cm)

FINISHED MEASUREMENTS

Block without border: 12 x 15in (30.5 x 38cm)
Block with border: 15 x 18in (38 x 45.5cm)

Chart color	Color key	Color name	Yarn required for 1 block	Yarn required for 4 blocks	Yarn required for 9 blocks	Yarn required for 16 blocks
●	MC	Light Gray	180yd (165m)	720yd (658m)	1620yd (1481m)	2880yd (2633m)
●	CC1	Charcoal or Black	110yd (101m)	440yd (402m)	990yd (905m)	1760yd (1609m)
●	CC2	Red	30yd (27m)	120yd (110m)	270yd (247m)	480yd (439m)
●	CC3	White	20yd (18m)	80yd (73m)	180yd (165m)	320yd (293m)
●	CC4	Black	2yd (2m)	8yd (7m)	18yd (16.5m)	32yd (29m)
●	CC5	Green or Yellow	2yd (2m)	8yd (7m)	18yd (16.5m)	32yd (29m)
●	CC6	Petal Pink	2yd (2m)	8yd (7m)	18yd (16.5m)	32yd (29m)

Block

Work in rows using the Intarsia colorwork technique (see Special Stitches). For the background, use **MC** from a skein and wind 1 butterfly-bobbin. For the cat head, use **CC1** from a skein.

To beg: With **MC** from skein – ch 45

Row 1: (RS) Dc in fourth ch from hook (the skipped chs count as dc), dc in each ch across; turn = 43 sts

Rows 2 – 10: Ch 2 (counts as dc now and throughout), skip first st, dc in each st across; turn = 43 sts

With RS facing, place **Marker** in the center stitch of the row just made to indicate the bottom edge of the head. Continue to work in rows, changing colors through the final stage of a stitch before new color indication.

Row 11: (RS) With **MC** from skein – ch 2, skip first st, dc in next 5 sts, dc2tog changing to **CC1** from skein; with **CC1** – 2 dc in next st, dc in next 25 sts, 2 dc in next st changing to **MC** from butterfly-bobbin; with **MC** – dc2tog, dc in next 6 sts; turn = 43 sts

Rows 12 – 14: With **MC** – ch 2, skip first st, dc in each st until 2 sts left before color change, dc2tog changing to **CC1**; with **CC1** – 2 dc in next st, dc in each st until 1 st left before color change, 2 dc in next st changing to **MC**; with **MC** – dc2tog, dc in each st to the end; turn = 43 sts

Rows 15 – 22: With **MC** – ch 2, skip first st, dc in next 3 sts changing to **CC1**; with **CC1** – dc in next 35 sts changing to **MC**; with **MC** – dc in next 4 sts; turn = 43 sts

Rows 23 – 26: With **MC** – ch 2, skip first st, dc in each st until 1 st left before color change, 2 dc in next st changing to **CC1**; with **CC1** – dc2tog, dc in each st until 2 sts left before color change, dc2tog changing to **MC**; with **MC** – 2 dc in next st, dc in each st to the end; turn = 43 sts

Break off **CC1** and **MC** from the butterfly-bobbin, and use **MC** from the skein for the rest of the block.

Rows 27 – 32: With **MC** – ch 2, skip first st, dc in each st across; turn = 43 sts

Do not fasten off, work 3 rnds of Granny Square Border with **MC** (see Penguin Block).

Bow

Optional – Make 1. Same as Bow in Monkey Block using **CC2**.

Ears

Make 2. Work in rows with **CC1**.

To beg: Ch 2

Row 1: (RS) 3 sc in second ch from hook (the skipped ch does not count as a st); turn = 3 sts

Row 2: (WS) Ch 1 (does not count as a st now and throughout), 2 sc in first st, 3 sc in next st, 2 sc in last st; turn = 7 sts

Row 3: (RS) Ch 1, 2 sc in first st, sc in next 2 sts, 3 sc in next st, sc in next 2 sts, 2 sc in last st; turn = 11 sts

Row 4: (WS) Ch 1, 2 sc in first st, sc in next 4 sts, 3 sc in next st, sc in next 4 sts, 2 sc in last st; turn = 15 sts

Row 5: (RS) Ch 1, 2 sc in first st, sc in next 6 sts, 3 sc in next st, sc in next 6 sts, 2 sc in last st; do not turn = 19 sts

Row 6: (RS) Ch 1, skip first st, rsc in next 17 sts, sl st in last st = 18 sts

Fasten off, leaving a long tail for sewing.

Nose

Make 1. Work in the round with **CC6**.

To beg: Ch 4

Rnd 1: Sc in second ch from hook (the skipped ch does not count as a st), sc in next ch, 3 sc in last ch; work across the opposite side of the foundation ch – (hdc, dc, hdc) in next ch, 2 sc in last ch; join = 10 sts

Fasten off, leaving a long tail for sewing.

Ear

Nose

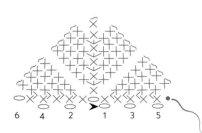

Block

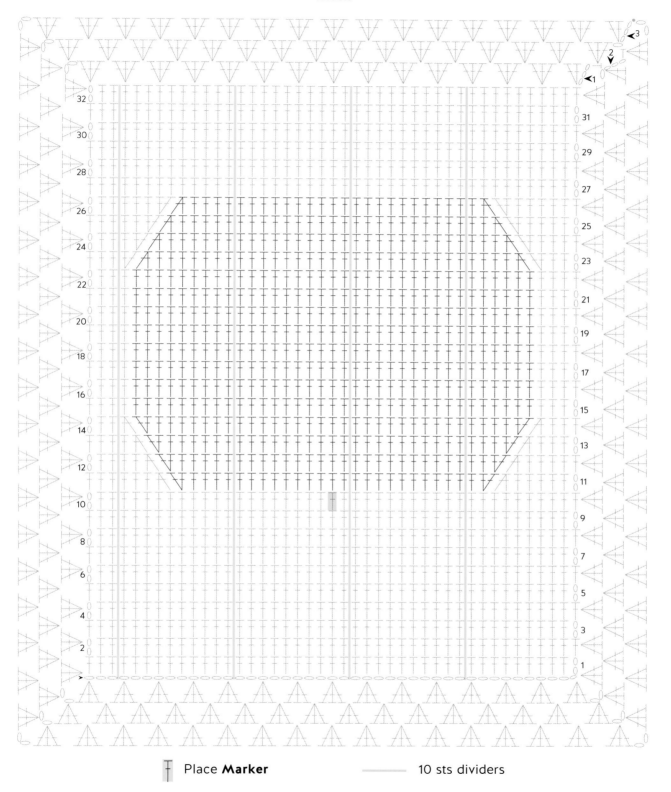

╥ Place **Marker**   ——— 10 sts dividers

Whiskers

Make 2 sets of whiskers. Work in rows with **CC1**.

Row 1: (RS) Ch 11, sl st in second ch from hook (the skipped ch does not count as a st), sl st in each ch across; do not turn = 10 sts

Rows 2 – 4: Same as Row 1

Fasten off, leaving a long tail for sewing.

Paws

Optional – Make 2. Work in the round with **CC1**.

To beg: Ch 8

Rnd 1: Sc in second ch from hook (the skipped ch does not count as a st), sc in next 5 chs, 3 sc in last ch; work across the opposite side of the foundation ch – sc in next 5 chs, 2 sc in last ch; join = 16 sts

Rnd 2: Ch 1 (does not count as a st now and throughout), 2 sc in same st as join, sc in next 5 sts, 2 sc in each of next 3 sts, sc in next 5 sts, 2 sc in each of next 2 sts; join = 22 sts

Rnd 3: Ch 1, 2 sc in same st as join, sc in next 7 sts, 2 sc in next st, skip st, 5 dc in next st, sl st in next st; [skip st, 5 dc in next st, skip st, sl st in next st] 2 times; 5 dc in next st, skip last st; join = 11 sc and 4 shells

Fasten off, leaving a long tail for sewing.

Eyes

Make 2. Begin by working in the round with **CC4**.

INNER EYE

To beg: With **CC4** – ch 3, sl st in third ch from hook to form a ring (or start with a magic ring)

Rnd 1: Ch 1 (does not count as a st), 8 hdc in ring; join and fasten off = 8 sts

Rnd 2: With **CC5** – beg sc in any st, sc in same st, 2 sc in each st around; join = 16 sts

Fasten off, leaving a long **CC5** tail for sewing. Thread the needle with **CC3** and stitch a highlight (fig 1).

OUTER EYE

To beg: With **CC3** – ch 3, sl st in third ch from hook to form a ring (or start with a magic ring)

Rnd 1: Ch 2 (does not count as a st), 12 dc in ring; join = 12 sts

Rnd 2: Ch 1 (does not count as a st now and throughout), 2 sc in same st as join, 2 sc in each of next 3 sts, skip st, (hdc, dc, tr) in next st, (tr, dc, hdc) in next st, skip st, 2 sc in each of next 4 sts; join = 22 sts

Rnd 3: Ch 1, sc in same st as join, sc in next 9 sts, 2 sc in each of next 2 sts, sc in next 10 sts; join = 24 sts

Fasten off, leaving a long tail for sewing.

FINISHING EYES

Position the inner eyes by the narrow end of the outer eyes, making sure that both highlights are facing in the same direction and backstitch around onto the outer eye with **CC5** tails (fig 2). Finish off and weave in the ends.

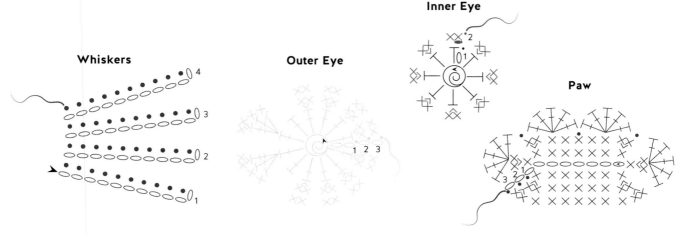

Whiskers

Outer Eye

Inner Eye

Paw

Finishing Block

Depending on the joining method and your project, you can finish the face before or after joining blocks (see Joining Blocks).

Position the nose 2 rows above the **Marker** on the block and backstitch around onto the block using **CC6** tail from the nose. With the same yarn, chain stitch a line across the center, from the nose to the bottom edge of the head (fig 2). Finish off, weave in the end and remove the marker.

Position the eyes 4 rows above the bottom edge on each side of the head, with the narrow edges facing to the center. Using **CC3** tail from each eye, backstitch around onto the block; finish off and weave in the ends (fig 2).

Place the whiskers 3 rows above the edge on each side of the head. For symmetry, one of the whisker sets should be with WS facing. Using **CC1** tail from the whiskers, whipstitch across the raw edge onto the block, leaving the edges around the whiskers unstitched (fig 2). Finish off and weave in the ends.

Position the ears on each side of the head, facing them towards the corners of the block. Using **CC1** tail from each ear, whipstitch across the bottom edge and backstitch around the remaining edges onto the block (fig 3). Finish off and weave in the ends.

Optional – Position the paws at a 45 degree angle below the head, with the toes facing up or down (figs 3 and 4). Using **CC1** tail from each paw, backstitch around onto the block. Finish off and weave in the ends.

Optional – Position the bow by the ear or under the chin and whipstitch across the top and bottom edges using the long **CC2** tail from each side (fig 4). Finish off and weave in the ends.

1

2

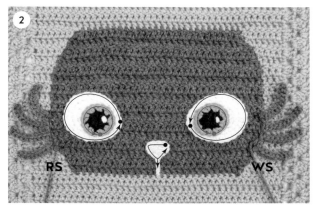

3

4

Sheep Block

Like a dreamy woolly cloud, a soft sheep blanket will warm you up and soothe your heart. Accent flowers will make your project even sweeter.

MATERIALS

To make this block, use your favorite medium weight acrylic yarn (weight 4) and a 5mm (H) hook or any hook size needed to obtain the gauge (see Tools and Materials). Use the table below to determine the amount required of each color yarn.

GAUGE

14 dc x 8.5 rows = 4 x 4in (10 x 10cm)

FINISHED MEASUREMENTS

Block without border: 12 x 15in (30.5 x 38cm)
Block with border: 15 x 18in (38 x 45.5cm)

Tip

Why not make a farmyard-themed blanket by combining this design with the Cow and Pig Blocks. Depending on the size of your blanket, Cat and Horse Blocks will be good additions as well.

Chart color	Color key	Color name	Yarn required for 1 block	Yarn required for 4 blocks	Yarn required for 9 blocks	Yarn required for 16 blocks
	MC	Yellow or Pink	180yd (165m)	720yd (658m)	1620yd (1481m)	2880yd (2633m)
	CC1	Light Gray	60yd (55m)	240yd (220m)	540yd (494m)	960yd (878m)
	CC2	White	60yd (55m)	240yd (220m)	540yd (494m)	960yd (878m)
	CC3	Jazzy	25yd (23m)	100yd (91m)	225yd (206m)	400yd (366m)
	CC4	Tea Leaf	5yd (4.5m)	20yd (18m)	45yd (41m)	80yd (73m)
	CC5	Black	5yd (4.5m)	20yd (18m)	45yd (41m)	80yd (73m)

Block

Work in rows using the Intarsia colorwork technique (see Special Stitches). For the background, use **MC** from a skein and wind 1 butterfly-bobbin. For the sheep head, use **CC1** from a skein. For the sheep hair, use **CC2** from a skein.

To beg: With **MC** from skein – ch 45

Row 1: (RS) Dc in fourth ch from hook (the skipped chs count as dc), dc in each ch across; turn = 43 sts

Rows 2 – 6: Ch 2 (counts as dc now and throughout), skip first st, dc in each st across; turn = 43 sts

With RS facing, place **Marker** in the center stitch of the row just made to indicate the bottom edge of the head. Continue to work in rows, changing colors through the final stage of a stitch before new color indication.

Row 7: (RS) With **MC** from skein – ch 2, skip first st, dc in next 7 sts, dc2tog changing to **CC1** from skein; with **CC1** – 2 dc in next st, dc in next 21 sts, 2 dc in next st changing to **MC** from butterfly-bobbin; with **MC** – dc2tog, dc in next 8 sts; turn = 43 sts

Rows 8 – 12: With **MC** – ch 2, skip first st, dc in each st until 2 sts left before color change, dc2tog changing to **CC1**; with **CC1** – 2 dc in next st, dc in each st until 1 st left before color change, 2 dc in next st changing to **MC**; with **MC** – dc2tog, dc in each st to the end; turn = 43 sts

Rows 13 – 16: With **MC** – ch 2, skip first st, dc in next 3 sts changing to **CC1**; with **CC1** – dc in next 35 sts changing to **MC**; with **MC** – dc in next 4 sts; turn = 43 sts

Break off **CC1** but continue using **MC**.

Row 17: (RS) With **MC** – ch 2, skip first st, dc in next st, dc2tog changing to **CC2** from skein; with **CC2** – 2 dc in next st, dc in each st until 1 st left before color change, 2 dc in next st changing to **MC**; with **MC** – dc2tog, dc in next 2 sts; turn = 43 sts

Row 18: (WS) With **MC** – ch 2, skip first st, dc in next 2 sts changing to **CC2**; with **CC2** – dc-lp in each of next 37 sts changing to **MC**; with **MC** – dc in next 3 sts; turn = 43 sts

Row 19: (RS) With **MC** – ch 2, skip first st, dc2tog changing to **CC2**; with **CC2** – 2 dc in next st, dc in each st until 1 st left before color change, 2 dc in next st changing to **MC**; with **MC** – dc2tog, dc in next st; turn = 43 sts

Row 20: (WS) With **MC** – ch 2, skip first st, dc in next st changing to **CC2**; with **CC2** – dc-lp in each of next 39 sts changing to **MC**; with **MC** – dc in next 2 sts; turn = 43 sts

Row 21: (RS) With **MC** – ch 2, skip first st, dc in next st changing to **CC2**; with **CC2** – dc in next 39 sts changing to **MC**; with **MC** – dc in next 2 sts; turn = 43 sts

Rows 22 – 23: Repeat Rows 20 - 21

Row 24: Same as Row 20

Row 25: (RS) With **MC** – ch 2, skip first st, 2 dc in next st changing to **CC2**; with **CC2** – dc2tog, dc in each st until 2 sts left before color change, dc2tog changing to **MC**; with **MC** – 2 dc in next st, dc in last st; turn = 43 sts

Row 26: Same as Row 18

Break off **CC2** and **MC** from the butterfly-bobbin, and use **MC** from the skein for the rest of the block.

Rows 27 – 32: With **MC** – ch 2, skip first st, dc in each st across; turn = 43 sts

Do not fasten off, work 3 rnds of Granny Square Border with **MC** (see Penguin Block).

Eyes

Make 2. Same as Eyes in Pig Block using **CC5** for the eyes and **CC2** for highlights.

Block

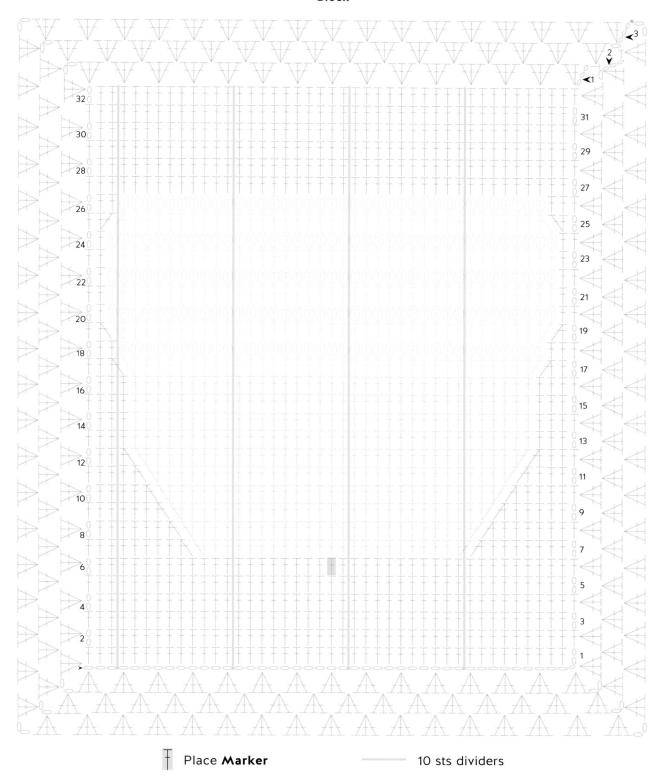

32 31
30 29
28 27
26 25
24 23
22 21
20 19
18 17
16 15
14 13
12 11
10 9
8 7
6 5
4 3
2 1

Place **Marker**   10 sts dividers

Ears

Make 2. Work in rows with **CC1**.

To beg: Ch 14

Row 1: (RS) Dc in fourth ch from hook (the skipped chs count as dc), dc in next 9 chs, 6 dc in last ch; work across the opposite side of the foundation ch – dc in next 11 chs; turn = 28 sts

Row 2: (WS) Ch 2 (counts as dc), skip first st, dc in next 10 sts, 2 dc in each of next 6 sts, dc in next 11 sts; turn = 34 sts

Row 3: (RS) Ch 1 (does not count as a st), sc in first st, sc in each st across = 34 sts

Fasten off, leaving a long tail for sewing. Fold the ear in half and whipstich across the bottom edge (fig 1). Do not weave in the end yet.

Flower

Optional – Make 1. Work in the round with **CC3**.

To beg: Ch 3, sl st in third ch from hook to form a ring (or start with a magic ring)

Rnd 1: Ch 1 (does not count as a st), 6 sc in ring; join = 6 sts

Rnd 2: Beg PC in same st as join, ch 2, [PC in next st, ch 2] 5 times; join = 6 PC

Rnd 3: [Ch 6, sc in second ch from hook, sc in next ch, hdc in next 2 chs, dc in last ch, sc in next ch-2 sp; ch 6, sc in second ch from hook, sc in next ch, hdc in next 2 chs, dc in last ch, sl st in next PC] 6 times = 12 petals

Fasten off, leaving a long tail for sewing.

Leaves

Optional – Make 1 set of 3 leaves. Work in rows with **CC4**.

Row 1: (RS) Ch 8, sl st in second ch from hook (the skipped ch does not count as a st), sc in next ch, hdc in next ch, dc in next 2 chs, hdc in next ch, sc in last ch; do not turn = 7 sts

Rows 2 – 3: Same as Row 1

Fasten off, leaving a long tail for sewing.

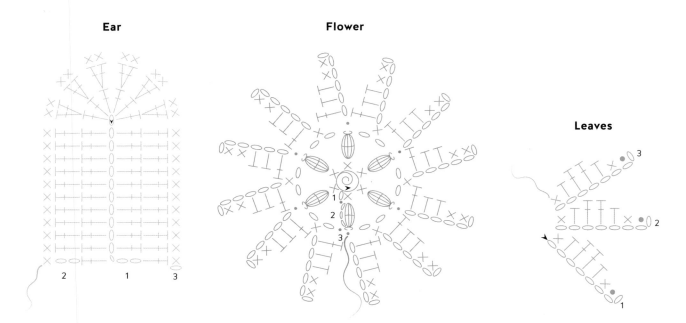

Ear

Flower

Leaves

Finishing Block

Depending on the joining method and your project, you can finish the face before or after joining blocks (see Joining Blocks).

Thread the needle with **CC5** and chain stitch a Y-shaped nose on the block just above the **Marker** (fig 2). Finish off, weave in the ends and remove the marker.

Position the eyes 4 rows above the bottom edge of the head and 3 sts away from the side edges. Using **CC5** tail from each eye, backstitch around onto the block (fig 3); finish off and weave in the ends.

Position the ears on each side of the head, just below the loops with their folded sides facing outwards. Using **CC1** tail from each ear, whipstitch across the seamed edge onto the block (fig 3). Finish off and weave in the ends.

Optional – Position the flower in one of the corners as you like and backstitch around the center onto the block using **CC3** tail (fig 4). Position the leaves under petals of the flower and whipstitch across the raw edge onto the block with **CC4** tail (fig 4). Finish off and weave in the ends.

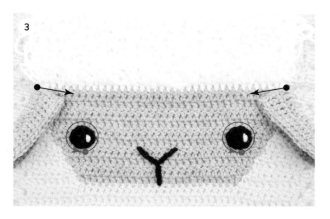

Tip

You can make a few flowers using different colors and place them randomly on the background of your finished blanket.

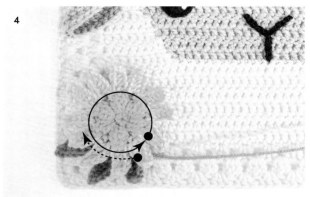

Sloth Block

You can nap all day and sleep all night under a soft, sleepy sloth blanket. Because when it's sloth o'clock, life is always mellow.

MATERIALS

To make this block, use your favorite medium weight acrylic yarn (weight 4) and a 5mm (H) hook or any hook size needed to obtain the gauge (see Tools and Materials). Use the table below to determine the amount required of each color yarn.

GAUGE

14 dc x 8.5 rows = 4 x 4in (10 x 10cm)

FINISHED MEASUREMENTS

Block without border: 12 x 15in (30.5 x 38cm)
Block with border: 15 x 18in (38 x 45.5cm)

Tip

Make a few pretty flowers for your sloth blanket, to sleep well and have beautiful dreams. Variegated yarn is a great choice for flowers, but you can also use different colors for the center and petals.

Chart color	Color key	Color name	Yarn required for 1 block	Yarn required for 4 blocks	Yarn required for 9 blocks	Yarn required for 16 blocks
	MC	Goldenrod	180yd (165m)	720yd (658m)	1620yd (1481m)	2880yd (2633m)
	CC1	Café Latte	100yd (91m)	400yd (366m)	900yd (823m)	1600yd (1463m)
	CC2	Buff	30yd (27m)	120yd (110m)	270yd (247m)	480yd (439m)
	CC3	Coffee	30yd (27m)	120yd (110m)	270yd (247m)	480yd (439m)
	CC4	Jazzy	25yd (23m)	100yd (91m)	225yd (206m)	400yd (366m)
	CC5	Tea Leaf	15yd (14m)	60yd (55m)	135yd (123m)	240yd (220m)

Block

Work in rows using the Intarsia colorwork technique (see Special Stitches). For the background, use **MC** from a skein and wind 1 butterfly-bobbin. For the sloth head, use **CC1** from a skein.

To beg: With **MC** from skein – ch 45

Row 1: (RS) Dc in fourth ch from hook (the skipped chs count as dc), dc in each ch across; turn = 43 sts

Rows 2 – 8: Ch 2 (counts as dc now and throughout), skip first st, dc in each st across; turn = 43 sts

With RS facing, place **Marker** in the center stitch of the row just made to indicate the bottom edge of the head. Continue to work in rows, changing colors through the final stage of a stitch before new color indication.

Row 9: (RS) With **MC** from skein – ch 2, skip first st, dc in next 5 sts, dc2tog changing to **CC1** from skein; with **CC1** – 2 dc in next st, dc in next 25 sts, 2 dc in next st changing to **MC** from butterfly-bobbin; with **MC** – dc2tog, dc in next 6 sts; turn = 43 sts

Rows 10 – 12: With **MC** – ch 2, skip first st, dc in each st until 2 sts left before color change, dc2tog changing to **CC1**; with **CC1** – 2 dc in next st, dc in each st until 1 st left before color change, 2 dc in next st changing to **MC**; with **MC** – dc2tog, dc in each st to the end; turn = 43 sts

Rows 13 – 20: With **MC** – ch 2, skip first st, dc in next 3 sts changing to **CC1**; with **CC1** – dc in next 35 sts changing to **MC**; with **MC** – dc in next 4 sts; turn = 43 sts

Rows 21 – 24: With **MC** – ch 2, skip first st, dc in each st until 1 st left before color change, 2 dc in next st changing to **CC1**; with **CC1** – dc2tog, dc in each st until 2 sts left before color change, dc2tog changing to **MC**; with **MC** – 2 dc in next st, dc in each st to the end; turn = 43 sts

Break off **CC1** and **MC** from the butterfly-bobbin, and use **MC** from the skein for the rest of the block.

Rows 25 – 32: With **MC** – ch 2, skip first st, dc in each st across; turn = 43 sts

Do not fasten off, work 3 rnds of Granny Square Border with **MC** (see Penguin Block).

Branch

Make 1. Work in rows with **CC5**.

To beg: Ch 4

Row 1: (RS) Sc in second ch from hook (the skipped ch does not count as a st), sc in next 2 chs; turn = 3 sts

Row 2: Ch 1 (does not count as a st now and throughout), sc in first st, sc in next 2 sts; turn = 3 sts

Row 3: Ch 8, sl st in second ch from hook, sc in next ch, hdc in next ch, dc in next 2 chs, hdc in next ch, sc in last ch; sc in next 3 sts; turn = 10 sts

Rows 4 – 5: Repeat Rows 2 – 3

Rows 6 – 7: Same as Row 2

Rows 8 – 25: Repeat Rows 2 – 7 three more times

Fasten off, leaving a long tail for sewing.

Branch

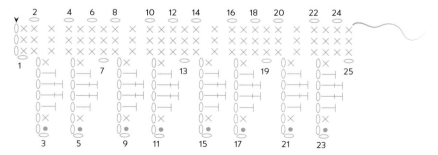

Block

Place **Marker**   ——— 10 sts dividers

Eye Patches

Make 2. Work in the round with **CC3**.

To beg: Ch 10

Rnd 1: Sc in second ch from hook (the skipped ch does not count as a st), sc in next 7 chs, 3 sc in last ch; work across the opposite side of the foundation ch – sc in next 7 chs, 2 sc in last ch; join = 20 sts

Rnd 2: Ch 1 (does not count as a st now and throughout), 2 sc in same st as join, sc in next 7 sts, 2 sc in each of next 3 sts, sc in next 7 sts, 2 sc in each of next 2 sts; join = 26 sts

Rnd 3: Ch 1, sc in same st as join, 2 sc in next st, sc in next 7 sts, [sc in next st, 2 sc in next st] 3 times, sc in next 7 sts, [sc in next st, 2 sc in next st] 2 times; join = 32 sts

Fasten off, leaving a long tail for sewing. Thread the needle with **CC2** and chain stitch a line across the foundation row on RS to represent sleepy eyes (fig 1). Finish off and weave in the end.

Paws

Make 2. Begin by working in the round with **CC1**.

To beg: With **CC1** – ch 9

Rnd 1: Dc in third ch from hook (the skipped chs do not count as a st), dc in next 5 chs, 6 dc in last ch; work across the opposite side of the foundation ch – dc in next 5 chs, 5 dc in last ch; join = 22 sts

Rnd 2: Sc in same st as join, sc in next 6 sts, 2 sc in each of next 4 sts, sc in next 7 sts, 2 sc in each of next 4 sts; join changing to **CC2**; fasten off **CC1** leaving a long tail for sewing = 30 sts

Row 3: With **CC2** – skip st with join, [ch 6, sc in second ch from hook, sc in next ch, hdc in next 2 chs, dc in last ch, skip next st, sl st in next st] 3 times (leave the remaining sts unworked) = 3 claws

Fasten off, leaving a long tail for sewing. You should have 2 long tails (**CC1** and **CC2**).

Face

Make 1. Work in the round with **CC2**.

To beg: Ch 13

Rnd 1: Dc in third ch from hook (the skipped chs do not count as a st), dc in next 9 chs, 6 dc in last ch; work across the opposite side of the foundation ch – dc in next 9 chs, 5 dc in last ch; join = 30 sts

Rnd 2: Ch 2 (does not count as a st now and throughout), 2 dc in same st as join, dc in next 9 sts, 2 dc in each of next 6 sts, dc in next 9 sts, 2 dc in each of next 5 sts; join = 42 sts

Rnd 3: Ch 2, dc in same st as join, 2 dc in next st, dc in next 9 sts, [dc in next st, 2 dc in next st] 6 times, dc in next 9 sts, [dc in next st, 2 dc in next st] 5 times; join = 54 sts

Rnd 4: Ch 2, 2 dc in same st as join, dc in next 11 sts, [2 dc in next st, dc in next 2 sts] 6 times, dc in next 9 sts, [2 dc in next st, dc in next 2 sts] 5 times; join = 66 sts

Fasten off, leaving a long tail for sewing.

Paw

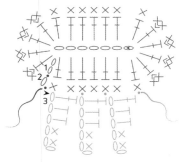

Face

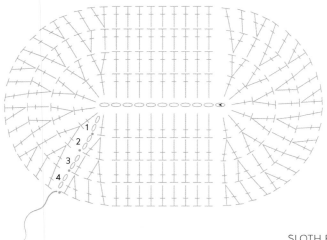

Eye Patch

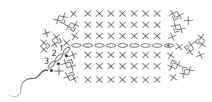

Nose

Make 1. Same as Nose in Fox Block using **CC3**.

Flower & Leaves

Optional – Make 1. Same as Flower and Leaves in Sheep Block using **CC4** for the flower and **CC5** for leaves.

Finishing Block

Depending on the joining method and your project, you can finish the face before or after joining blocks (see Joining Blocks).

Position the face on the block, centering it 3 rows above the **Marker** and backstitch around onto the block using **CC2** tail from the face (fig 2). Finish off and weave in the end.

Position the nose in the center of the face and backstitch around onto the face using **CC3** tail from the nose (fig 2). Finish off and weave in the ends.

Position the eye patches on each side of the head, placing them at a slight angle over the head and covering the face. Using **CC3** tail from each eye patch, backstitch around onto the block (fig 3). Finish off and weave in the ends.

Position the branch below the head, centering it with the **Marker** and remove the marker. Backstitch around onto the block using **CC5** tail, leaving the leaves unstitched (fig 3). Finish off and weave in the ends.

Thread the needle with **CC3** and stitch a V-shaped smile on the face 1 rnd below the nose (fig 4). Finish off and weave in the ends.

Position the paws on each side of the branch, placing them at a slight angle. Using **CC1** tail from each paw, backstitch around onto the block, then backstitch around the claws using **CC2** tail (fig 4). Finish off and weave in the ends.

Optional – Position the flower as you like and backstitch around the center onto the block using **CC4** tail (fig 4). Position the leaves under petals of the flower and whipstitch across the raw edge onto the block with **CC5** tail (fig 4). Finish off and weave in the ends.

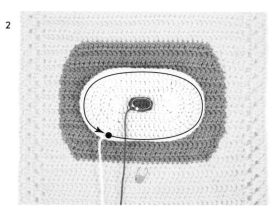

Lion Block

· · · · · · · · · · · · ·

A roaring lion blanket with matching cushions will transform your home into a jungle, and you can add some accent bows for extra cuteness.

MATERIALS

To make this block, use your favorite medium weight acrylic yarn (weight 4) and a 5mm (H) hook or any hook size needed to obtain the gauge (see Tools and Materials). Use the table below to determine the amount required of each color yarn.

GAUGE

14 dc x 8.5 rows = 4 x 4in (10 x 10cm)

FINISHED MEASUREMENTS

Block without border: 12 x 15in (30.5 x 38cm)
Block with border: 15 x 18in (38 x 45.5cm)

Tip

· · · · · · · · · · · · ·

You can use this block along with the Hippo Block and the Monkey Block to create a cute jungle blanket that will bring a safari into your home.

Chart color	Color key	Color name	Yarn required for 1 block	Yarn required for 4 blocks	Yarn required for 9 blocks	Yarn required for 16 blocks
●	MC	Forest Green	180yd (165m)	720yd (658m)	1620yd (1481m)	2880yd (2633m)
●	CC1	Gold	110yd (101m)	440yd (402m)	990yd (905m)	1760yd (1609m)
●	CC2	Lemon Yellow	35yd (32m)	140yd (128m)	315yd (288m)	560yd (512m)
●	CC3	Carrot	15yd (14m)	60yd (55m)	135yd (123m)	240yd (220m)
●	CC4	Coffee	5yd (4.5m)	20yd (18m)	45yd (41m)	80yd (73m)
●	CC5	White	1yd (1m)	4yd (4m)	9yd (8.5m)	16yd (15m)

Block

Work in rows using the Intarsia colorwork technique (see Special Stitches). For the background, use **MC** from a skein and wind 1 butterfly-bobbin. For the lion head, use **CC1** from a skein.

To beg: With **MC** from skein – ch 45

Row 1: (RS) Dc in fourth ch from hook (the skipped chs count as dc), dc in each ch across; turn = 43 sts

Rows 2 – 6: Ch 2 (counts as dc now and throughout), skip first st, dc in each st across; turn = 43 sts

With RS facing, place **Marker** in the center stitch of the row just made to indicate the bottom edge of the head. Continue to work in rows, changing colors through the final stage of a stitch before new color indication.

Row 7: (RS) With **MC** from skein – ch 2, skip first st, dc in next 5 sts, dc2tog changing to **CC1** from skein; with **CC1** – 2 dc in next st, dc in next 25 sts, 2 dc in next st changing to **MC** from butterfly-bobbin; with **MC** – dc2tog, dc in next 6 sts; turn = 43 sts

Row 8: (WS) With **MC** – ch 2, skip first st, dc in next 4 sts, dc2tog changing to **CC1**; with **CC1** – 2 dc-lp in next st, dc-lp in each of next 5 sts, dc in next 17 sts, dc-lp in each of next 5 sts, 2 dc-lp in next st changing to **MC**; with **MC** – dc2tog, dc in next 5 sts; turn = 43 sts

Row 9: (RS) With **MC** – ch 2, skip first st, dc in next 3 sts, dc2tog changing to **CC1**; with **CC1** – 2 dc in next st, dc in next 29 sts, 2 dc in next st changing to **MC**; with **MC** – dc2tog, dc in next 4 sts; turn = 43 sts

Row 10: (WS) With **MC** – ch 2, skip first st, dc in next 2 sts, dc2tog changing to **CC1**; with **CC1** – 2 dc-lp in next st, dc-lp in each of next 5 sts, dc in next 21 sts, dc-lp in each of next 5 sts, 2 dc-lp in next st changing to **MC**; with **MC** – dc2tog, dc in next 3 sts; turn = 43 sts

Row 11: (RS) With **MC** – ch 2, skip first st, dc in next 3 sts changing to **CC1**; with **CC1** – dc in next 35 sts changing to **MC**; with **MC** – dc in next 4 sts; turn = 43 sts

Row 12: (WS) With **MC** – ch 2, skip first st, dc in next 3 sts changing to **CC1**; with **CC1** – dc-lp in each of next 7 sts, dc in next 21 sts, dc-lp in each of next 7 sts changing to **MC**; with **MC** dc in next 4 sts; turn = 43 sts

Rows 13 – 18: Repeat Rows 11 - 12 three more times

Row 19: Same as Row 11

Row 20: (WS) With **MC** – ch 2, skip first st, dc in each st to next color and change to **CC1**; with **CC1** – dc-lp in each st to next color and change to **MC**; with **MC** – dc in each st to the end; turn = 43 sts

Row 21: (RS) With **MC** – ch 2, skip first st, dc in each st until 1 st left before color change, 2 dc in next st changing to **CC1**; with **CC1** – dc2tog, dc in each st until 2 sts left before color change, dc2tog changing to **MC**; with **MC** – 2 dc in next st, dc in each st to the end; turn = 43 sts

Rows 22 – 25: Repeat Rows 20 - 21 two more times

Row 26: Same as Row 20

Break off **CC1** and **MC** from the butterfly-bobbin, and use **MC** from the skein for the rest of the block.

Rows 27 – 32: With **MC** – ch 2, skip first st, dc in each st across; turn = 43 sts

Do not fasten off, work 3 rnds of Granny Square Border with **MC** (see Penguin Block).

Ears

Make 2. Work in rows with **CC1**.

To beg: Ch 3, sl st in third ch from hook to form a ring (or start with a magic ring)

Row 1: (WS) Ch 2 (counts as dc now and throughout), 6 dc in ring; turn = 7 sts

Row 2: (RS) Ch 2, dc in first st, 2 dc in each of next 6 sts; do not turn = 14 sts

Row 3: (RS) Ch 1 (does not count as a st), skip first st, rsc in next 12 sts, sl st in last st = 13 sts

Fasten off, leaving a long tail for sewing.

Ear

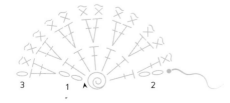

3   1   2

Block

Place **Marker**   ——— 10 sts dividers

Muzzle

Make 1. Work in the round with **CC2**.

To beg: Ch 18

Rnd 1: Sc in second ch from hook (the skipped ch does not count as a st), sc in next 15 chs, 3 sc in last ch; work across the opposite side of the foundation ch − sc in next 15 chs, 2 sc in last ch; join = 36 sts

Rnd 2: Ch 1 (does not count as a st now and throughout), 2 sc in same st as join, sc in next 6 sts, sc3tog, sc in next 6 sts, 2 sc in each of next 3 sts, sc in next 7 sts, 3 sc in next st, sc in next 7 sts, 2 sc in each of next 2 sts; join = 42 sts

Rnd 3: Ch 1, sc in same st as join, 2 sc in next st, sc in next 5 sts, sc3tog, sc in next 5 sts; [2 sc in next st, sc in next st] 3 times; sc in next 8 sts, 3 sc in next st, sc in next 9 sts; 2 sc in next st, sc in next st, 2 sc in last st; join = 48 sts

Rnd 4: Ch 1, 2 sc in same st as join, sc in next 6 sts, sc3tog, sc in next 6 sts, 2 sc in next st; [sc in next 2 sts, 2 sc in next st] 2 times; sc in next 9 sts, 3 sc in next st, sc in next 9 sts; [2 sc in next st, sc in next 2 sts] 2 times; join = 54 sts

Rnd 5: Ch 1, sc in same st as join, sc in next 2 sts, 2 sc in next st, sc in next 3 sts, sc3tog, sc in next 3 sts; [2 sc in next st, sc in next 3 sts] 2 times; 2 sc in next st, sc in next 13 sts, 3 sc in next st, sc in next 13 sts, 2 sc in next st, sc in next 3 sts, 2 sc in last st; join = 60 sts

Fasten off, leaving a long tail for sewing.

Bow

Optional − Make 1. Begin by working in the round with **CC3**.

To beg: Ch 3, sl st in third ch from hook to form a ring (or start with a magic ring)

Rnd 1: Ch 1 (does not count as a st now and throughout), 8 hdc in ring; join = 8 sts

Work in rows from now on:

Row 2: Ch 1, sc in same st as join, sc in next 2 sts; *skip st and place **Marker** in next st**; turn = 3 sts

Row 3: Ch 1, 2 sc in first st, sc in next st, 2 sc in last st; turn = 5 sts

Row 4: Ch 1, sc in first st, sc in next 4 sts; turn = 5 sts

Row 5: Ch 1, 2 sc in first st, sc in next 3 sts, 2 sc in last st; turn = 7 sts

Row 6: (RS) Ch 1, sc in first st, sc in next 6 sts = 7 sts

Fasten off and weave in the ends.

With RS facing, join **CC3** in st with **Marker** and repeat Rows 2 − 6, omitting the instructions from * to **.

Remove the marker and continue to work edging with RS facing − Ch 1, sc evenly around the entire edge, placing 3 sc in corners for increasing; join.

Fasten off and weave in the ends.

To complete the bow, cut a long piece of **CC3** and wrap it around the center multiple times (fig 1). Finish off, leaving a long tail for sewing.

Muzzle

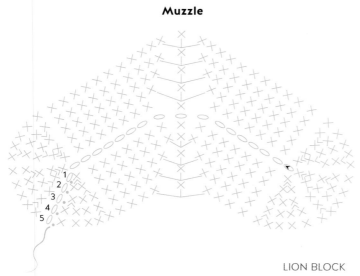

Bow

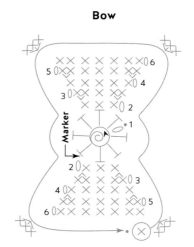

Eyes

Make 2. Same as Eyes in Pig Block using **CC4** for the eyes and **CC5** for highlights.

Nose

Make 1. Same as Nose in Fox Block using **CC4**.

Finishing Block

Depending on the joining method and your project, you can finish the face before or after joining blocks (see Joining Blocks).

With the pointy edge of the muzzle facing upwards, position the nose just below the top edge and backstitch around the muzzle using **CC4** tail from the nose, then chain stitch from the nose down to the bottom edge of the muzzle (fig 2). Finish off and weave in the end.

Position the muzzle on the head, centering the bottom edge of the muzzle right above the **Marker** on the block. Using **CC2** tail from the muzzle, backstitch around onto the block (fig 2). Finish off, weave in the end and remove the marker.

Position the eyes on each side of the muzzle, placing them right up against the muzzle. Using **CC4** tail from each eye, backstitch around onto the block (fig 2). Finish off and weave in the ends.

Position the ears on each side of the head, just inside the mane edge. Using **CC1** tail from each ear, whip-stitch across the bottom edge onto the block, leaving the remaining edges unstitched (fig 3). Finish off and weave in the ends.

Optional – Position the bow under the muzzle and backstitch around the center onto the block with **CC3** tail, leaving the sides unstitched (fig 4). Finish off and weave in the end.

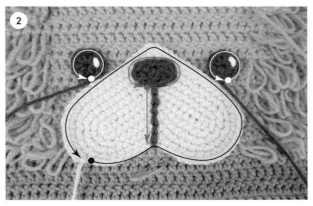

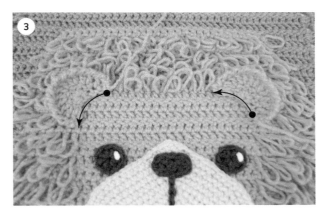

Raccoon Block

· · · · · · · · · · · · · ·

Nothing can beat the happiness of reading a book under the covers. A gaze of raccoons on a cute blanket will keep you safe while you're getting cozy with a good story.

MATERIALS

To make this block, use your favorite medium weight acrylic yarn (weight 4) and a 5mm (H) hook or any hook size needed to obtain the gauge (see Tools and Materials). Use the table below to determine the amount required of each color yarn.

GAUGE

14 dc x 8.5 rows = 4 x 4in (10 x 10cm)

FINISHED MEASUREMENTS

Block without border: 12 x 15in (30.5 x 38cm)
Block with border: 15 x 18in (38 x 45.5cm)

Tip

· · · · · · · · · · · · · ·

To add extra cuteness, use one Fox Block in your raccoon blanket as an accent, or you could alternate the Raccoon and Fox Blocks in your project.

Chart color	Color key	Color name	Yarn required for 1 block	Yarn required for 4 blocks	Yarn required for 9 blocks	Yarn required for 16 blocks
●	MC	Teal Heather or Pink	180yd (165m)	720yd (658m)	1620yd (1481m)	2880yd (2633m)
●	CC1	Gray Heather	75yd (69m)	300yd (274m)	675yd (617m)	1200yd (1097m)
●	CC2	Black	50yd (46m)	200yd (183m)	450yd (411m)	800yd (732m)
●	CC3	White	30yd (27m)	120yd (110m)	270yd (247m)	480yd (439m)

Block

Same as Fox Block, but omit markers in Row 11. Work with **MC**, **CC1** and **CC2**.

Ears

Make 2. Work in rows starting with **CC2**.

To beg: With **CC2** – ch 5

Row 1: (WS) Sc in second ch from hook (the skipped ch does not count as a st), sc in next 2 chs, (2 sc, ch 1, 2 sc) in last ch; work across the opposite side of the foundation ch – sc in next 3 chs; turn = 10 sts

Row 2: (RS) Ch 1 (does not count as a st now and throughout), sc in first st, sc in next 4 sts, (2 sc, ch 1, 2 sc) in next ch-1 sp, sc in next 5 sts; turn = 14 sts

Row 3: (WS) Ch 1, sc in first st, sc in next 6 sts, (2 sc, ch 1, 2 sc) in next ch-1 sp, sc in next 7 sts; change to **CC1**, break off **CC2** and turn = 18 sts

Row 4: (RS) With **CC1** – ch 1, sc in first st, sc in next 8 sts, 3 sc in next ch-1 sp, sc in next 9 sts; do not turn = 21 sts

Row 5: (RS) Ch 1, skip first st, rsc in next 19 sts, sl st in last st = 20 sts

Fasten off, leaving a long tail for sewing.

Muzzle

Make 1. Same as Ears in Pig Block using **CC3**.

Eyes

Make 2. Same as Inner Eyes in Cat Block using **CC2** to begin and change to **CC3** in Rnd 2; add highlights with **CC3**.

Nose

Make 1. Work in the round with **CC2**.

To beg: Ch 4

Rnd 1: Sc in second ch from hook (the skipped ch does not count as a st), sc in next ch, 3 sc in last ch; work across the opposite side of the foundation ch – (hdc, dc, hdc) in next ch, 2 sc in last ch; join = 10 sts

Fasten off, leaving a long tail for sewing.

Eyebrows

Make 2. Work in rows with **CC3**.

To beg: Ch 22

Row 1: (WS) Sc in second ch from hook (the skipped ch does not count as a st), sc in each ch across; turn = 21 sts

Row 2: (RS) Ch 1 (does not count as a st), sc in first st, sc in next st, picot, [sc in next 2 sts, picot] 9 times, sc in last st = 21 sts and 10 picots

Fasten off, leaving a long tail for sewing.

Ear

Nose

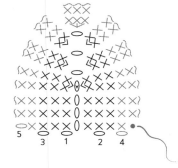

Eyebrow

Finishing Block

Depending on the joining method and your project, you can finish the face before or after joining blocks (see Joining Blocks).

With the pointy edge of the muzzle facing upwards, position it in the center of the head, lining up the bottom edge with the face edge. Using the long **CC3** tail from the muzzle, backstitch around onto the block (fig 1). Finish off and weave in the end.

Position the eyebrows along the side edges of the face. For right-handed crochet, the long tails from eyebrows will be on the top right and on the bottom left sides. For left-handed crochet, the tails will be in the reversed order. Using the long **CC3** tail from each eyebrow, whipstitch across the inner edge onto the block and backstitch around the remaining edges (fig 1). Finish off and weave in the ends.

Position the ears on each side of the head, facing them towards the corners of the block. Using **CC1** tail from each ear, whipstitch across the bottom edge onto the block and backstitch around the remaining edges (fig 2). Finish off and weave in the ends.

With the pointy edge of the nose facing down, position it just above the center of the muzzle. Using the long **CC2** tail from the nose, backstitch around onto the muzzle (fig 2). Finish off and weave in the end.

Position the eyes on each side of the muzzle and backstitch around onto the block using **CC3** tail from each eye (fig 2). Finish off and weave in the ends.

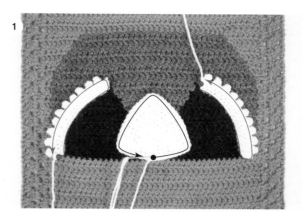

Cow Block

Your sweet little farmers will be over the moon about their very own cow blanket. With a sunflower decoration, this blanket is the perfect addition to a summer picnic.

MATERIALS

To make this block, use your favorite medium weight acrylic yarn (weight 4) and a 5mm (H) hook or any hook size needed to obtain the gauge (see Tools and Materials). Use the table below to determine the amount required of each color yarn.

GAUGE

14 dc x 8.5 rows = 4 x 4in (10 x 10cm)

FINISHED MEASUREMENTS

Block without border: 12 x 15in (30.5 x 38cm)
Block with border: 15 x 18in (38 x 45.5cm)

Chart color	Color key	Color name	Yarn required for 1 block	Yarn required for 4 blocks	Yarn required for 9 blocks	Yarn required for 16 blocks
●	MC	Spring Green	180yd (165m)	720yd (658m)	1620yd (1481m)	2880yd (2633m)
●	CC1	White	80yd (73m)	320yd (293m)	720yd (658m)	1280yd (1170m)
●	CC2	Rosy	30yd (27m)	120yd (110m)	270yd (247m)	480yd (439m)
●	CC3	Black	30yd (27m)	120yd (110m)	270yd (247m)	480yd (439m)
●	CC4	Bright Yellow	20yd (18m)	80yd (73m)	180yd (165m)	320yd (293m)
●	CC5	Coffee	10yd (9m)	40yd (37m)	90yd (82m)	160yd (146m)
●	CC6	Buff	10yd (9m)	40yd (37m)	90yd (82m)	160yd (146m)
●	CC7	Pine	3yd (3m)	12yd (11m)	27yd (25m)	48yd (44m)
●	CC8	Turqua	3yd (3m)	12yd (11m)	27yd (25m)	48yd (44m)
●	CC9	Carrot	2yd (2m)	8yd (7m)	18yd (16.5m)	32yd (29m)

Block

Work in rows using the Intarsia colorwork technique (see Special Stitches). For the background, use **MC** from a skein and wind 1 butterfly-bobbin. For the cow head, use **CC1** from a skein.

To beg: With **MC** from skein – ch 45

Row 1: (RS) Dc in fourth ch from hook (the skipped chs count as dc), dc in each ch across; turn = 43 sts

Rows 2 – 6: Ch 2 (counts as dc now and throughout), skip first st, dc in each st across; turn = 43 sts

With RS facing, place **Marker** in the center stitch of the row just made to indicate the bottom edge of the head. Continue to work in rows, changing colors through the final stage of a stitch before new color indication.

Row 7: (RS) With **MC** from skein – ch 2, skip first st, dc in next 9 sts, dc2tog changing to **CC1** from skein; with **CC1** – 2 dc in next st, dc in next 17 sts, 2 dc in next st changing to **MC** from butterfly-bobbin; with **MC** – dc2tog, dc in next 10 sts; turn = 43 sts

Rows 8 – 14: With **MC** – ch 2, skip first st, dc in each st until 2 sts left before color change, dc2tog changing to **CC1**; with **CC1** – 2 dc in next st, dc in each st until 1 st left before color change, 2 dc in next st changing to **MC**; with **MC** – dc2tog, dc in each st to the end; turn = 43 sts

Rows 15 – 24: With **MC** – ch 2, skip first st, dc in next 3 sts changing to **CC1**; with **CC1** – dc in next 35 sts changing to **MC**; with **MC** – dc in next 4 sts; turn = 43 sts

Rows 25 – 26: With **MC** – ch 2, skip first st, dc in each st until 1 st left before color change, 2 dc in next st changing to **CC1**; with **CC1** – dc2tog, dc in each st until 2 sts left before color change, dc2tog changing to **MC**; with **MC** – 2 dc in next st, dc in each st to the end; turn = 43 sts

Break off **CC1** and **MC** from the butterfly-bobbin, and use **MC** from the skein for the rest of the block.

Rows 27 – 32: With **MC** – ch 2, skip first st, dc in each st across; turn = 43 sts

Do not fasten off, work 3 rnds of Granny Square Border with **MC** (see Penguin Block).

Muzzle

Make 1. Work in the round with **CC2**.

To beg: Ch 15

Rnd 1: Dc in third ch from hook (the skipped chs do not count as a st), dc in next 5 chs, 3 dc in next ch, dc in next 5 chs, 6 dc in last ch; work across the opposite side of the foundation ch – dc in next 4 chs, dc3tog, dc in next 4 chs, 5 dc in last ch; join = 34 sts

Rnd 2: Ch 2 (does not count as a st now and throughout), 2 dc in same st as join, dc in next 6 sts, 3 dc in next st, dc in next 6 sts, 2 dc in each of next 6 sts, dc in next 3 sts, dc3tog, dc in next 3 sts, 2 dc in each of next 5 sts; join = 46 sts

Rnd 3: Ch 2, dc in same st as join, 2 dc in next st, dc in next 7 sts, 3 dc in next st, dc in next 7 sts, [2 dc in next st, dc in next st] 6 times, dc in next 2 sts, dc3tog, dc in next 2 sts, [dc in next st, 2 dc in next st] 5 times; join = 58 sts

Fasten off, leaving a long tail for sewing.

Nostrils

Make 2. Same as Nostrils in Hippo Block using **CC6**. Position the nostrils on each side of the muzzle in Rnd 1 and backstitch around using **CC6** tails (fig 2). Finish off and weave in the ends.

Eyes

Make 2. Same as Eyes in Dog Block using **CC3** for inner eyes, **CC8** for outer eyes and **CC1** for highlights.

Muzzle

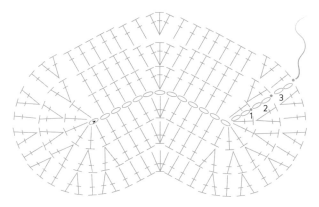

Block

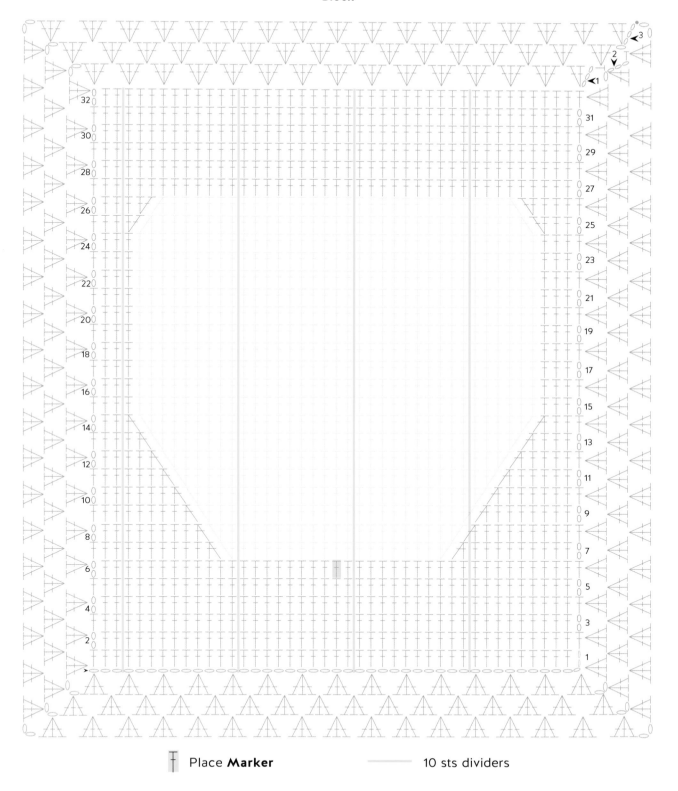

$\top$ Place **Marker**   ——— 10 sts dividers

COW BLOCK

-79-

Ears

Make 2. Work in rows with **CC3**.

To beg: Ch 10

Row 1: (RS) Dc in fourth ch from hook (the skipped chs count as dc), dc in next 5 chs, 6 dc in last ch; work across the opposite side of the foundation ch – dc in next 7 chs; turn = 20 sts

Row 2: (WS) Ch 2 (counts as dc), skip first st, dc in next 6 sts, 2 dc in each of next 6 sts, dc in next 7 sts; turn = 26 sts

Row 3: (RS) Ch 1 (does not count as a st), sc in first st, sc in each st across = 26 sts

Fasten off, leaving a long tail for sewing. Fold the sides of the ear towards the center and whipstitch across the bottom edge (fig 1). Do not weave in the end yet.

Horns

Make 2. Work in rows with **CC6**.

To beg: Ch 7

Row 1: (WS) Sc in second ch from hook (the skipped ch does not count as a st), sc in next 4 chs, 3 sc in last ch; work across the opposite side of the foundation ch – sc in next 5 chs; turn = 13 sts

Row 2: (RS) Ch 1 (does not count as a st), sc in first st, sc in next 4 sts, 2 sc in each of next 3 sts, sc in next 5 sts = 16 sts

Fasten off, leaving a long tail for sewing.

Spot

Make 1. Work in the round with **CC3**.

To beg: Ch 3, sl st in third ch from hook to form a ring (or start with a magic ring)

Rnd 1: Ch 1 (does not count as a st now and throughout), [sc in ring, ch 4, sc in second ch from hook, sc in next 2 chs] 3 times; join = 12 sts

Rnd 2: Ch 1, sc in same st as join, sc in next 3 sts across the foundation ch, 2 sc in turning ch, sc in next 3 sts, [sc in next st, sc in next 3 sts across the foundation ch, 2 sc in turning ch, sc in next 3 sts] 2 times; join = 27 sts

Fasten off, leaving a long tail for sewing.

Flower

Optional – Make 1. Work in the round starting with **CC5**.

To beg: With **CC5** – ch 3, sl st in third ch from hook to form a ring (or start with a magic ring)

Rnd 1: Ch 1 (does not count as a st now and throughout), 6 sc in ring; join = 6 sts

Rnd 2: Beg PC in same st as join, ch 2, [PC in next st, ch 2] 5 times; join = 6 PC and 6 ch-2 sps

Rnd 3: Ch 1, [sc in PC, 3 sc in next ch-2 sp] 6 times; join, changing to **CC4**; break off **CC5** = 24 sts

Rnd 4: With **CC4** – ch 1, sc in same st as join, sc in next st, (sc, ch 8, sc) in next st, [sc in next 3 sts, (sc, ch 8, sc) in next st] 5 times, sc in last st; join = 30 sts and 6 loops

Rnd 5: Skip st with join, *skip next 2 sts; work in loop – (6 dc, ch 3, sl st in third ch from hook, 6 dc), skip 2 sts, sl st in next st; repeat 5 more times from * = 6 petals

Fasten off, leaving a long **CC4** tail for sewing.

Flower

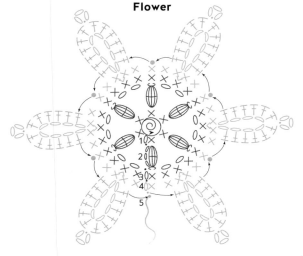

Ear

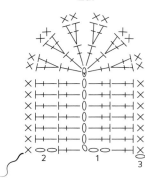

Leaf

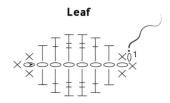

Leaf

Optional – Make 1. Work in the round with **CC7**.

To beg: Ch 9

Rnd 1: Sc in second ch from hook (the skipped ch does not count as a st), *hdc in next ch, dc in next ch, tr in next 2 chs, dc in next ch, hdc in next ch**, 3 sc in last ch; work across the opposite side of the foundation ch – repeat from * to **, 2 sc in last ch; join = 18 sts

Fasten off, leaving a long tail for sewing.

Center fold

Finishing Block

Depending on the joining method and your project, you can finish the face before or after joining blocks (see Joining Blocks).

Position the muzzle on the head with its pointy edge facing upwards, centering the bottom edge of the muzzle right above the **Marker** on the block.

Using **CC2** tail from the muzzle, backstitch around onto the block (fig 2). Finish off, weave in the end and remove the marker.

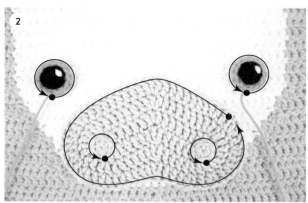

Position the eyes on each side of the muzzle, 3 sts away from the head edges and position the spot 2 rows above the right eye. Backstitch around each piece onto the block (figs 2 and 3). Finish off and weave in the ends.

Position the ears on each side of the head at a 45 degree angle and whipstitch across the seamed edge onto the block using the long **CC1** tail, then backstitch along the center of each ear (fig 3). Finish off and weave in the ends.

Position the horns on the top of the head, with 13 center sts between them. Using the long **CC6** tail from each horn, whipstitch across the bottom edge onto the block and backstitch around the remaining edges (fig 3). Finish off and weave in the ends.

Optional – Add 3 tassels on the top of the head using **CC9** (see Finishing Touches) and trim the ends. Position the flower by the left ear and backstitch around the center onto the block using **CC4** tail. Position the leaf under petals and backstitch around onto the block with **CC7** tail. Finish off and weave in the ends.

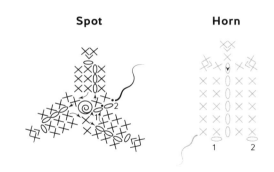

Spot   **Horn**

Unicorn Block

· · · · · · · · · · · · ·

You don't have to catch unicorns if you can crochet! With a blanket in your favorite colors, you just make your own magic!

MATERIALS

To make this block, use your favorite medium weight acrylic yarn (weight 4) and a 5mm (H) hook or any hook size needed to obtain the gauge (see Tools and Materials). Use the table below to determine the amount required of each color yarn.

GAUGE

14 dc x 8.5 rows = 4 x 4in (10 x 10cm)

FINISHED MEASUREMENTS

Block without border: 12 x 15in (30.5 x 38cm)
Block with border: 15 x 18in (38 x 45.5cm)

Tip

· · · · · · · · · · · · ·

Add a magical touch of color to your Unicorn Block by using a bright variegated yarn for the mane. Colorful spirals are simply delightful.

Chart color	Color key	Color name	Yarn required for 1 block	Yarn required for 4 blocks	Yarn required for 9 blocks	Yarn required for 16 blocks
●	MC	Light Jasmine or Petal Pink	180yd (165m)	720yd (658m)	1620yd (1481m)	2880yd (2633m)
○	CC1	White	100yd (91m)	400yd (366m)	900yd (823m)	1600yd (1463m)
●	CC2	Day Glow	40yd (37m)	160yd (146m)	360yd (330m)	640yd (585m)
○	CC3	Bright Yellow	30yd (27m)	120yd (110m)	270yd (247m)	480yd (439m)
○	CC4	Rosy	10yd (9m)	40yd (37m)	90yd (82m)	160yd (146m)
●	CC5	Gray Heather	2yd (2m)	8yd (7m)	18yd (16.5m)	32yd (29m)

Block

Work in rows using the Intarsia colorwork technique (see Special Stitches). For the background, use **MC** from a skein and wind 1 butterfly-bobbin. For the unicorn head, use **CC1** from a skein.

To beg: With **MC** from skein − ch 45

Row 1: (RS) Dc in fourth ch from hook (the skipped chs count as dc), dc in each ch across; turn = 43 sts

Rows 2 – 6: Ch 2 (counts as dc now and throughout), skip first st, dc in each st across; turn = 43 sts

With RS facing, place **Marker** in the center stitch of the row just made to indicate the bottom edge of the head. Continue to work in rows, changing colors through the final stage of a stitch before new color indication.

Row 7: (RS) With **MC** from skein − ch 2, skip first st, dc in next 10 sts, dc2tog changing to **CC1** from skein; with **CC1** − 2 dc in next st, dc in next 15 sts, 2 dc in next st changing to **MC** from butterfly-bobbin; with **MC** − dc2tog, dc in next 11 sts; turn = 43 sts

Rows 8 – 14: With **MC** − ch 2, skip first st, dc in each st until 2 sts left before color change, dc2tog changing to **CC1**; with **CC1** − 2 dc in next st, dc in each st until 1 st left before color change, 2 dc in next st changing to **MC**; with **MC** − dc2tog, dc in each st to the end; turn = 43 sts

Row 15: With **MC** − ch 2, skip first st, dc in next 4 sts changing to **CC1**; with **CC1** − dc in next 2 sts and place **Marker** in last st made, dc in next 9 sts and place **Marker** in last st made, dc in next 12 sts and place **Marker** in last st made, dc in next 9 sts and place **Marker** in last st made, dc in next st changing to **MC**; with **MC** − dc in next 5 sts; turn = 43 sts

Rows 16 – 24: With **MC** − ch 2, skip first st, dc in next 4 sts changing to **CC1**; with **CC1** − dc in next 33 sts changing to **MC**; with **MC** − dc in next 5 sts; turn = 43 sts

Rows 25 – 26: With **MC** − ch 2, skip first st, dc in each st until 1 st left before color change, 2 dc in next st changing to **CC1**; with **CC1** − dc2tog, dc in each st until 2 sts left before color change, dc2tog changing to **MC**; with **MC** − 2 dc in next st, dc in each st to the end; turn = 43 sts

Break off **CC1** and **MC** from the butterfly-bobbin, and use **MC** from the skein for the rest of the block.

Rows 27 – 32: With **MC** − ch 2, skip first st, dc in each st across; turn = 43 sts

Do not fasten off, work 3 rnds of Granny Square Border with **MC** (see Penguin Block).

Horn

Make 1. Work in rows with **CC3**.

To beg: Ch 16

Row 1: (WS) Sc in second ch from hook (the skipped ch does not count as a st), sc in next 13 chs, (2 sc, ch 1, 2 sc) in last ch; work across the opposite side of the foundation ch − sc in next 14 chs; turn = 32 sts

Row 2: (RS) Ch 2 (counts as dc), skip first st, dc in next 5 sts, hdc in next 6 sts, sc in next 4 sts, 3 sc in next ch-1 sp, sc in next 4 sts, hdc in next 6 sts, dc in next 6 sts; do not turn = 35 sts

Row 3: (RS) Ch 1 (does not count as a st), skip first st, rsc in next 33 sts, sl st in last st = 34 sts

Fasten off, leaving a long tail for sewing.

Horn

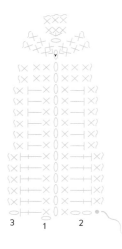

Block

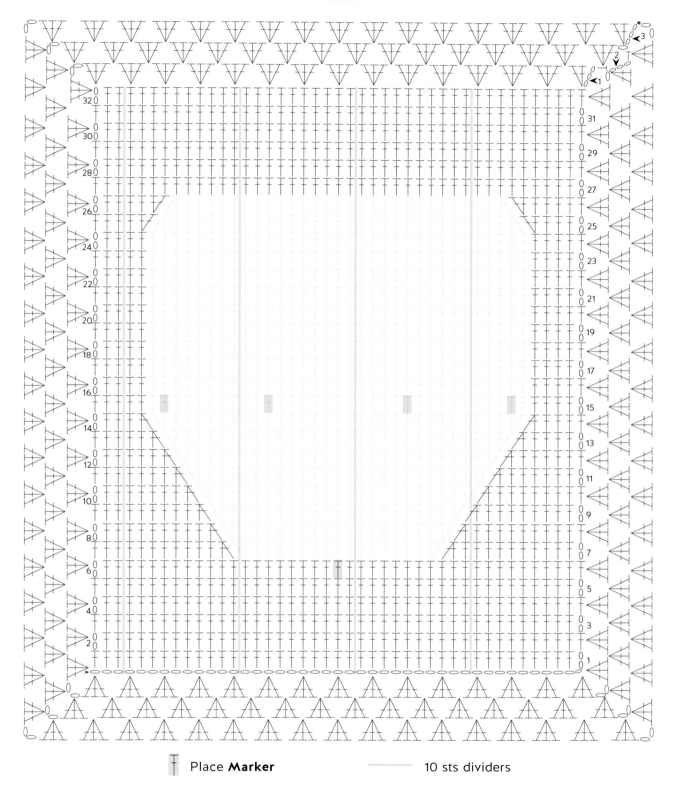

† Place **Marker**   ⎯⎯⎯ 10 sts dividers

Ears

Make 2. Work in rows with **CC1**.

To beg: Ch 5

Row 1: (RS) Sc in second ch from hook (the skipped ch does not count as a st), sc in next 2 chs, (2 sc, ch 1, 2 sc) in last ch; work across the opposite side of the foundation ch – sc in next 3 chs; turn = 10 sts

Row 2: (WS) Ch 1 (does not count as a st now and throughout), sc in first st, sc in next 4 sts, (2 sc, ch 1, 2 sc) in next ch-1 sp, sc in next 5 sts; turn = 14 sts

Row 3: (RS) Ch 1, sc in first st, sc in next 6 sts, 3 sc in next ch-1 sp, sc in next 7 sts; do not turn = 17 sts

Row 4: (RS) Ch 1, skip first st, rsc in next 15 sts, sl st in last st = 16 sts

Fasten off, leaving a long tail for sewing.

Cheeks

Make 2. Same as Cheeks in Panda Block using **CC4**.

Star

Make 1. Work in the round with **CC3**.

To beg: Ch 3, sl st in third ch from hook to form a ring (or start with a magic ring)

Rnd 1: Ch 2 (does not count as a st), 10 hdc in ring; join = 10 sts

Rnd 2: Ch 1 (does not count as a st), sc in same st as join, 2 sc in next st, [sc in next st, 2 sc in next st] 4 times; join = 15 sts

Rnd 3: Skip st with join, [ch 7, sl st in second ch from hook, sc in next ch, hdc in next 2 chs, dc in final 2 chs, skip 2 sts, sl st in next st] 5 times = 5 star points

Fasten off, leaving a long tail for sewing.

Mane

Make 1 long piece and 1 short piece. Work in rows with **CC2**.

SHORT PIECE

Row 1: Ch 16, 2 sc in second ch from hook (the skipped ch does not count as a st), 2 sc in each ch across; do not turn = 30 sts

Rows 2 – 5: Same as Row 1

Fasten off, leaving a long tail for sewing.

LONG PIECE

Row 1: Ch 16, 2 sc in second ch from hook (the skipped ch does not count as a st), 2 sc in each ch across; do not turn = 30 sts

Rows 2 – 8: Same as Row 1

Fasten off, leaving a long tail for sewing.

Mane

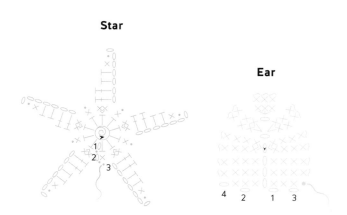

Star

Ear

Finishing Block

Depending on the joining method and your project, you can finish the face before or after joining blocks (see Joining Blocks).

Finish the eyes with **CC5** as follows: First Eye – make a slipknot and complete fpsc around the post of the st with first **Marker** in Row 15 of the Block, work fpsc in each st to next **Marker**; fasten off and weave in the ends. Second Eye – make a slipknot and complete fpsc around the post of the st with next **Marker**, work fpsc in each st to last **Marker**; fasten off and weave in the ends (fig 1). Remove the eye markers.

Position the cheeks on each side of the head, 2 rows above the row with center **Marker**. Using the long **CC4** tail from each cheek, backstitch around onto the block (fig 2). Finish off, weave in the ends and remove the marker.

Position the ears on each side of the head, right up against the top edge. Using the long **CC1** tail from each ear, whipstitch across the bottom edge onto the block and backstitch around the remaining edges (fig 2). Finish off and weave in the ends.

Position the horn in the center of the head between the ears, with its bottom edge 4 rows below the head edge. Using the long **CC3** tail from the horn, whipstitch across the bottom edge onto the block and backstitch around the remaining edges (fig 2). Finish off and weave in the end.

Position the long piece of the mane horizontally along the bottom edge of the horn to the head edge. Using the long **CC2** tail from the mane, whipstitch across the top edge onto the block (fig 3). Finish off and weave in the end.

Position the short piece of the mane horizontally above the long piece, placing it along the top edge of the head to the horn. Using the long **CC2** tail from the mane, whipstitch across the top edge onto the block (fig 3). Finish off and weave in the end.

Position the star on the opposite side from the mane and backstitch around onto the block using the long **CC3** tail from the star (fig 3). Finish off and weave in the end.

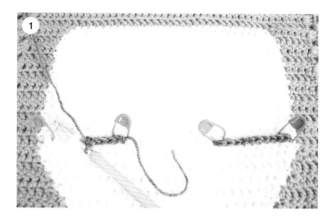

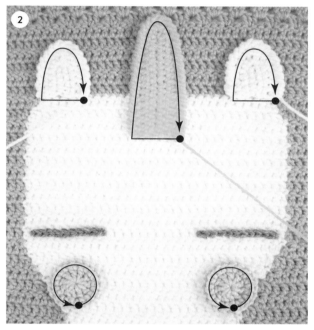

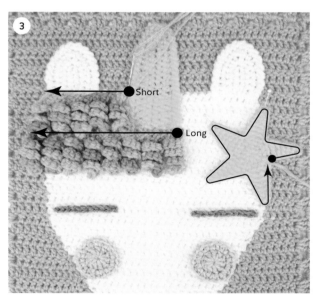

Bunny Block

· · · · · · · · · · · ·

Hop hop hippity hop, playful bunnies jump a lot! At the end of the day, your little some-bunny will enjoy nestling under a soft cozy blanket and will sleep better at night.

MATERIALS

To make this block, use your favorite medium weight acrylic yarn (weight 4) and a 5mm (H) hook or any hook size needed to obtain the gauge (see Tools and Materials). Use the table below to determine the amount required of each color yarn.

GAUGE

14 dc x 8.5 rows = 4 x 4in (10 x 10cm)

FINISHED MEASUREMENTS

Block without border: 12 x 15in (30.5 x 38cm)
Block with border: 15 x 18in (38 x 45.5cm)

Tip

· · · · · · · · · · · · ·

It's a great idea to use yarn scraps for the flowers and border. Granny Bunny is a fantastic stash-buster, it will help you to reduce your stash effectively.

Chart color	Color key	Color name	Yarn required for 1 block	Yarn required for 4 blocks	Yarn required for 9 blocks	Yarn required for 16 blocks
⬤	MC	Light Coral or Buff	180yd (165m)	720yd (658m)	1620yd (1481m)	2880yd (2633m)
⬤	CC1	Lemon Yellow	110yd (101m)	440yd (402m)	990yd (905m)	1760yd (1609m)
⬤	CC2	Natural	30yd (27m)	120yd (110m)	270yd (247m)	480yd (439m)
⬤	CC3	Café Latte	5yd (4.5m)	20yd (18m)	45yd (41m)	80yd (73m)
⬤	CC4	Orange	10yd (9m)	40yd (37m)	90yd (82m)	160yd (146m)
⬤	CC5	Neon Yellow	10yd (9m)	40yd (37m)	90yd (82m)	160yd (146m)

Block

Work in rows using the Intarsia colorwork technique (see Special Stitches). For the background, use **MC** from a skein and wind 1 butterfly-bobbin. For the bunny head, use **CC1** from a skein.

To beg: With **MC** from skein – ch 45

Row 1: (RS) Dc in fourth ch from hook (the skipped chs count as dc), dc in each ch across; turn = 43 sts

Rows 2 – 6: Ch 2 (counts as dc now and throughout), skip first st, dc in each st across; turn = 43 sts

With RS facing, place **Marker** in the center stitch of the row just made to indicate the bottom edge of the head. Continue to work in rows, changing colors through the final stage of a stitch before new color indication.

Row 7: (RS) With **MC** from skein – ch 2, skip first st, dc in next 3 sts, dc2tog changing to **CC1** from skein; with **CC1** – 2 dc in next st, dc in next 29 sts, 2 dc in next st changing to **MC** from butterfly-bobbin; with **MC** – dc2tog, dc in next 4 sts; turn = 43 sts

Row 8: (WS) With **MC** – ch 2, skip first st, dc in next 2 sts, dc2tog changing to **CC1**; with **CC1** – 2 dc in next st, dc in next 31 sts, 2 dc in next st changing to **MC**; with **MC** – dc2tog, dc in next 3 sts; turn = 43 sts

Rows 9 – 14: With **MC** – ch 2, skip first st, dc in next 3 sts changing to **CC1**; with **CC1** – dc in next 35 sts changing to **MC**; with **MC** – dc in next 4 sts; turn = 43 sts

Rows 15 – 22: With **MC** – ch 2, skip first st, dc in each st until 1 st left before color change, 2 dc in next st changing to **CC1**; with **CC1** – dc2tog, dc in each st until 2 sts left before color change, dc2tog changing to **MC**; with **MC** – 2 dc in next st, dc in each st to the end; turn = 43 sts

Break off **CC1** and **MC** from the butterfly-bobbin, and use **MC** from the skein for the rest of the block.

Rows 23 – 32: With **MC** – ch 2, skip first st, dc in each st across; turn = 43 sts

Do not fasten off, work 3 rnds of Granny Square Border with **MC** (see Penguin Block). For a more authentic granny square look, you can change colors in every round of the border.

Block

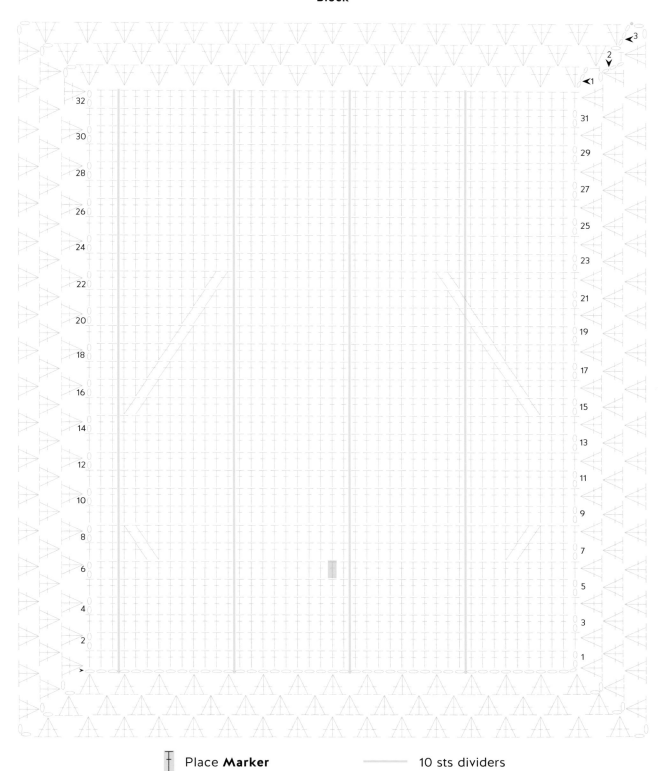

32
30
28
26
24
22
20
18
16
14
12
10
8
6
4
2

31
29
27
25
23
21
19
17
15
13
11
9
7
5
3
1

3
2
1

Place **Marker**   ──── 10 sts dividers

Muzzle

Make 1. Work in the round with **CC2**.

To beg: Ch 13

Rnd 1: Dc in third ch from hook (the skipped chs do not count as a st), dc in next 9 chs, 6 dc in last ch; work across the opposite side of the foundation ch – dc in next 9 chs, 5 dc in last ch; join = 30 sts

Rnd 2: Ch 2 (does not count as a st), 2 dc in same st as join, dc in next 9 sts, 2 dc in each of next 6 sts, dc in next 9 sts, 2 dc in each of next 5 sts; join = 42 sts

Rnd 3: Ch 1 (does not count as a st), sc in same st as join, sc in each st around; join = 42 sts

Fasten off, leaving a long tail for sewing.

Ears

Make 2. Work in rows with **CC1**.

To beg: Ch 16

Row 1: (RS) Sc in second ch from hook (the skipped ch does not count as a st), sc in next 4 chs, hdc in next 5 chs, dc in next 4 chs, 7 dc in last ch; work across the opposite side of the foundation ch – dc in next 4 chs, hdc in next 5 chs, sc in next 5 chs; turn = 35 sts

Row 2: (WS) Ch 1 (does not count as a st), sc in first st, sc in next 13 sts, 2 sc in each of next 3 sts, sc in next st, 2 sc in each of next 3 sts, sc in next 14 sts; turn = 41 sts

Row 3: (RS) Skip first st, [skip next st, 5 dc in next st, skip next st, sl st in next st] 10 times = 10 shells

Fasten off, leaving a long tail for sewing.

Flower

Optional – Make 3. Work in the round starting with **CC4** (**CC5**).

To beg: With **CC4** (**CC5**) – ch 3, sl st in third ch from hook to form a ring (or start with a magic ring)

Rnd 1: Ch 1 (does not count as a st), 6 sc in ring; join = 6 sts

Rnd 2: Beg PC in same st as join, ch 2, [PC in next st, ch 2] 5 times; join changing to **CC5** (**CC4**) = 6 PC and 6 ch-2 sps

Rnd 3: With **CC5** (**CC4**) – [6 dc in next ch-2 sp, sl st in next PC] 6 times = 6 petals

Fasten off, leaving a long **CC5** (**CC4**) tail for sewing.

Eyes

Make 2. Same as Eyes in Pig Block using **CC3** for the eyes and **CC2** for highlights.

Nose

Make 1. Same as Nose in Cat Block using **CC3**.

Ear

Muzzle

Flower

Finishing Block

Depending on the joining method and your project, you can finish the face before or after joining blocks (see Joining Blocks).

Position the muzzle horizontally on the head, centering it right above the **Marker** on the block. Using **CC2** tail from the muzzle, backstitch around onto the block (fig 1). Finish off, weave in the end and remove the marker.

Position the ears on the top of the head, slanting them slightly towards the corners of the block. Using the long **CC1** tail from each ear, whipstitch across the bottom edge onto the block and backstitch just under the shell edges (fig 1). Finish off and weave in the ends.

Position the nose just below the top edge of the muzzle in the center and backstitch around onto the muzzle using the long **CC3** tail (fig 2). Finish off and weave in the end.

Position the eyes on each side of the muzzle, placing them right up against the muzzle. Using **CC3** tail from each eye, backstitch around onto the block (fig 2). Finish off and weave in the ends.

Optional – Position 3 flowers as you like and backstitch around the center onto the block using the long **CC5** (**CC4**) tail from each flower (fig 3). Finish off and weave in the ends.

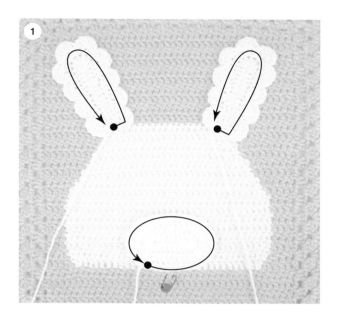

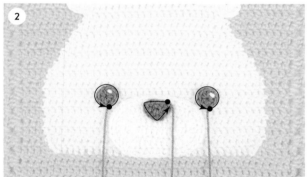

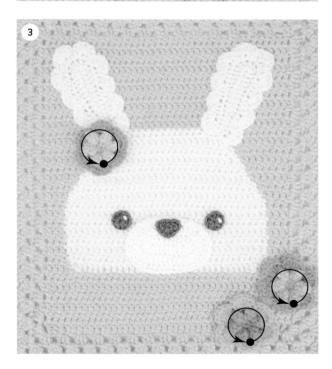

Fox Block

Being crafty like a fox will help you to finish a secret project for a special animal enthusiast. You can decorate your blocks with artful scarves in an assortment of colors.

MATERIALS

To make this block, use your favorite medium weight acrylic yarn (weight 4) and a 5mm (H) hook or any hook size needed to obtain the gauge (see Tools and Materials). Use the table below to determine the amount required of each color yarn.

GAUGE

14 dc x 8.5 rows = 4 x 4in (10 x 10cm)

FINISHED MEASUREMENTS

Block without border: 12 x 15in (30.5 x 38cm)

Block with border: 15 x 18in (38 x 45.5cm)

Tip

A silver fox on a teal background would make a perfect complementary block to a red fox. For a woodland theme, use this design along with the Raccoon, Bunny and Bear Blocks.

Chart color	Color key	Color name	Yarn required for 1 block	Yarn required for 4 blocks	Yarn required for 9 blocks	Yarn required for 16 blocks
●	MC	Light Gray	180yd (165m)	720yd (658m)	1620yd (1481m)	2880yd (2633m)
●	CC1	Carrot	75yd (69m)	300yd (274m)	675yd (617m)	1200yd (1097m)
●	CC2	White	50yd (46m)	200yd (183m)	450yd (411m)	800yd (732m)
●	CC3	Black	30yd (27m)	120yd (110m)	270yd (247m)	480yd (439m)
●	CC4	Teal Heather or Aqua	30yd (27m)	120yd (110m)	270yd (247m)	480yd (439m)

Block

Work in rows using the Intarsia colorwork technique (see Special Stitches). For the background, use **MC** from a skein and wind 1 butterfly-bobbin. For the fox face, use **CC2** from a skein and wind 1 butterfly-bobbin. For the fox head, use **CC1** from a skein and wind 2 butterfly-bobbins.

To beg: With **MC** from a skein – ch 45

Row 1: (RS) Dc in fourth ch from hook (the skipped chs count as dc), dc in each ch across; turn = 43 sts

Rows 2 – 8: Ch 2 (counts as dc now and throughout), skip first st, dc in each st across; turn = 43 sts

Continue to work in rows, changing colors through the final stage of a stitch before new color indication.

Rows 9 – 10: With **MC** from skein – ch 2, skip first st, dc in next st changing to **CC1** from skein; with **CC1** – dc in next st changing to **CC2** from skein; with **CC2** – dc in next 37 sts changing to **CC1** from butterfly-bobbin; with **CC1** – dc in next st changing to **MC** from butterfly-bobbin; with **MC** – dc in next 2 sts; turn = 43 sts

Row 11: (RS) With **MC** – ch 2, skip first st, dc in next st changing to **CC1**; with **CC1** – 2 dc in next st changing to **CC2**; *with **CC2** – dc2tog, dc in next 3 sts and place **Marker** in st just made, dc in next 9 sts and place **Marker** in st just made, dc in next 2 sts, dc2tog changing to **CC1** from butterfly-bobbin**; with **CC1** – 3 dc in next st changing to **CC2**; repeat from * to **; with **CC1** – 2 dc in next st changing to **MC**; with **MC** – dc in next 2 sts; turn = 43 sts

Row 12: (WS) With **MC** – ch 2, skip first st, dc in next st changing to **CC1**; with **CC1** – dc in next st, 2 dc in next st changing to **CC2**; *with **CC2** – dc2tog, dc in each st until 2 sts left before color change, dc2tog changing to **CC1**; with **CC1** – 2 dc in next st, dc in next st, 2 dc in next st changing to **CC2**; repeat from * to **; with **CC1** – 2 dc in next st, dc in next st changing to **MC**; with **MC** – dc in next 2 sts; turn = 43 sts

Rows 13 – 17: With **MC** – ch 2, skip first st, dc in next st changing to **CC1**; with **CC1** – dc in each st until 1 st left before color change, 2 dc in next st changing to **CC2**; *with **CC2** – dc2tog, dc in each st until 2 sts left before color change, dc2tog changing to **CC1**; with **CC1** – 2 dc in next st, dc in each st until 1 st left before color change, 2 dc in next st changing to **CC2**; repeat from * to **; with **CC1** – 2 dc in next st, dc in each st to next color and change to **MC**; with **MC** – dc in next 2 sts; turn = 43 sts

Row 18: (WS) With **MC** – ch 2, skip first st, dc in next st changing to **CC1**; with **CC1** – dc in next 7 sts, 2 dc in next st changing to **CC2**; *with **CC2** – [dc2tog] 2 times and change to **CC1**; with **CC1** – 2 dc in next st, dc in next 13 sts, 2 dc in next st changing to **CC2**; repeat from * to **; with **CC1** – 2 dc in next st, dc in next 7 sts changing to **MC**; with **MC** – dc in next 2 sts; turn = 43 sts

Break off **CC2** from the skein and butterfly-bobbin. Continue to work with **MC** and **CC1**.

Row 19: (RS) With **MC** – ch 2, skip first st, 2 dc in next st changing to **CC1**; with **CC1** – dc2tog, dc in each st until 2 sts left before color change, dc2tog changing to **MC**; with **MC** – 2 dc in next st, dc in last st; turn = 43 sts

Rows 20 – 24: With **MC** – ch 2, skip first st, dc in each st until 1 st left before color change, 2 dc in next st changing to **CC1**; with **CC1** – dc2tog, dc in each st until 2 sts left before color change, dc2tog changing to **MC**; with **MC** – 2 dc in next st, dc in each st to the end; turn = 43 sts

Break off **CC1** and **MC** from the butterfly-bobbin, and use **MC** from the skein for the rest of the block.

Rows 25 – 32: With **MC** – ch 2, skip first st, dc in each st across; turn = 43 sts

Do not fasten off, work 3 rnds of Granny Square Border with **MC** (see Penguin Block).

Block

$\dagger$ Place **Marker**   ———— 10 sts dividers

Ears

Make 2. Work in rows starting with **CC3**.

To beg: With **CC3** – ch 2

Row 1: (WS) 3 sc in second ch from hook (the skipped ch does not count as a st); turn = 3 sts

Row 2: (RS) Ch 1 (does not count as a st now and throughout), 2 sc in first st, 3 sc in next st, 2 sc in last st; turn = 7 sts

Row 3: (WS) Ch 1, 2 sc in first st, sc in next 2 sts, 3 sc in next st, sc in next 2 sts, 2 sc in last st; turn = 11 sts

Row 4: (RS) Ch 1, 2 sc in first st, sc in next 4 sts, 3 sc in next st, sc in next 4 sts, 2 sc in last st = 15 sts

Row 5: (WS) Ch 1, 2 sc in first st, sc in next 6 sts, 3 sc in next st, sc in next 6 sts, 2 sc in last st changing to **CC1**; break off **CC3** and turn = 19 sts

Row 6: (RS) With **CC1** – ch 1, 2 sc in first st, sc in next 8 sts, 3 sc in next st, sc in next 8 sts, 2 sc in last st; do not turn = 23 sts

Row 7: (RS) Ch 1, skip first st, rsc in next 21 sts, sl st in last st = 22 sts

Fasten off, leaving a long tail for sewing.

Whiskers

Make 2 sets of whiskers. Work in rows with **CC1**.

Row 1: (RS) Ch 11, 2 sc in second ch from hook (the skipped ch does not count as a st), 2 sc in each ch across; do not turn = 20 sts

Rows 2 – 3: Same as Row 1

Fasten off, leaving a long tail for sewing.

Nose

Make 1. Work in the round with **CC3**.

To beg: Ch 5

Rnd 1: Sc in second ch from hook (the skipped ch does not count as a st), sc in next 2 chs, 3 sc in last ch; work across the opposite side of the foundation ch – sc in next 2 chs, 2 sc in last ch; join = 10 sts

Fasten off, leaving a long tail for sewing.

Scarf

Optional – Make 1. Work in rows with **CC4**.

To beg: Ch 25

Row 1: (WS) Sc in second ch from hook (the skipped ch does not count as a st), sc in each ch across; turn = 24 sts

Rows 2 – 3: Ch 2 (counts as dc), skip first st, x-dc across to last st, dc in last st; turn = 11 x-dc and 2 dc

Row 4: (RS) Ch 1 (does not count as a st), sc in first st, sc in each st across; turn = 24 sts

Row 5: (WS) Skip first st, [ch 17, dc in fourth ch from hook, dc in next 13 chs, skip st, sl st in next st] 2 times; leave the remaining sts unworked = 2 strips

Fasten off, leaving a long tail for sewing.

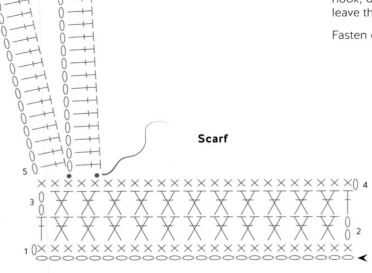

Scarf

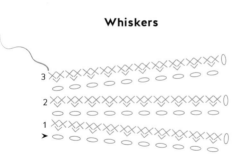

Whiskers

Finishing Block

Depending on the joining method and your project, you can finish the face before or after joining blocks (see Joining Blocks).

To finish the eyes, work with **CC3** from **Marker** to **Marker** on each side of the face, removing markers as you go: Make a slipknot and complete fpsc around the post of the st with first **Marker**, fpsc in each st to next **Marker** (fig 1). Fasten off and weave in the ends.

Position the nose in the center just above the face edge and backstitch around onto the block using **CC3** tail (fig 2). Finish off and weave in the end.

Place the whiskers on each side of the head above the bottom edge. For symmetry, one of the whisker sets should be with WS facing. Using **CC1** tail from each of the whisker sets, whipstitch across the raw edge onto the block, leaving the spirals unstitched (fig 2). Finish off and weave in the ends.

Position the ears on each side of the head, facing them towards the corners of the block. Using **CC1** tail from each ear, whipstitch across the bottom edge and backstitch around the remaining edges onto the block (fig 3). Finish off and weave in the ends.

Optional – Position the scarf in the center of the block below the nose, with the long strips facing upwards on the left side of the scarf (or on the right side for left-handed crochet). Using **CC4** tail from the scarf, backstitch around the edge onto the block, leaving the strips unstitched (fig 4). Fold the strips down after sewing. Finish off and weave in the ends.

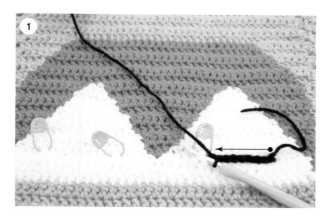

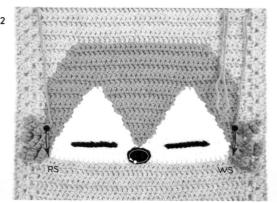

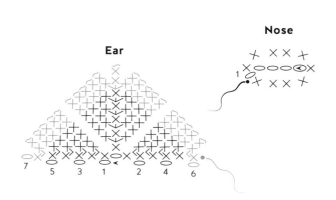

Ear

Nose

Additional Ideas

. . . .

Mix 'n' Match Animals

Expand your imagination while having fun! You can mix and match elements from different blocks to create new animals. For example, here are a few simple steps for making a Bear and a Horse.

HORSE BLOCK

Make the **Unicorn** block using Light Sage for the background and Chocolate Tweed for the head. From the **Unicorn** pattern, make 2 ears using Chocolate Tweed, make 2 mane pieces using Black, and make 1 horn using Buff to represent the patch. From the **Bunny** pattern, make 1 muzzle using Buff. From the **Dog** pattern, make 2 outer eyes using Black and stitch highlights with White, then make 2 pupils using Chocolate Tweed to represent nostrils. Assemble all pieces as shown in fig 1.

BEAR BLOCK

Make the **Sloth** block using Botany Teal for the background and Café Latte for the head. From the **Fox** pattern, make 1 nose using Coffee. From the **Bunny** pattern, make 1 muzzle using Oatmeal. From the **Pig** pattern, make 2 eyes using Coffee and stitch highlights with White. From the **Lion** pattern, make 2 ears using Café Latte. Assemble all pieces as shown in fig 2.

Plain Block

Plain blocks are great fillers and they are fast to make. You can use them in a blanket between animal blocks or as a back side of your project. Use 1 color for the entire block or change colors every row using 3 different colors.

Begin with ch 45 and finish the first row of any animal block. Work rows 2 – 32 without a face: Ch 2 (counts as dc), skip first st, dc in each st across; turn = 43 sts. Do not fasten off, work 3 rnds of Granny Square Border (see Penguin Block).

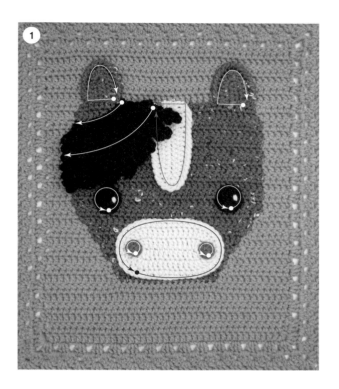

Project Ideas

Incorporate your animal blocks into blankets, cushions, storage bags and more. You can even use each block individually as a wall hanging or a doll blanket, the possibilities are endless. This section of the book provides you with instructions and some project ideas, so you can create the thing you wish existed.

Blanket Without Border

. . . .

A special handmade blanket is a meaningful family heirloom which can also be passed down to future generations. Make a blanket or make a few to keep your whole family warm and cozy. Use your favorite animal blocks or arrange the blocks with different animals into your very own unique blanket.

To finish a blanket without border, make 4 blocks for a small blanket (S), 9 blocks for a medium blanket (M) or 16 blocks for a large blanket (L).

Join blocks using your favorite method (see Joining Blocks). If you join-as-you-go (JAYGO), sew animal faces onto each block after joining that block to the previously made block(s). For other joining methods, sew animal faces onto each block before joining them.

There are no additional yarn requirements for a blanket without border; you will only need the yarn listed in animal blocks.

SIZES

Blanket Size	Measurements	Number of Blocks
Small (S)	30 x 36in (76 x 91cm)	4
Medium (M)	45 x 54in (114 x 137cm)	9
Large (L)	60 x 72in (152 x 180cm)	16

Your blanket is finished once you assemble the blocks, but if you wish, you can also add a border around the entire edge of your blanket (see Granny Square Border and Shell Border).

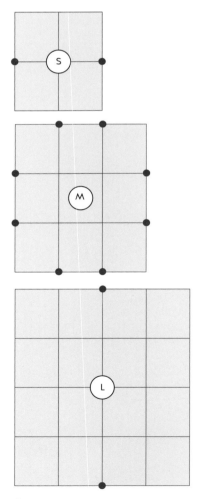

● = Place **Marker** (for blanket with shell border only)

Granny Square Border

· ·

To enlarge your blanket, add a simple granny square border using yarn in complementary colors.

SIZES AND YARN

Measurements and Yarn	Small Blanket (S)	Medium Blanket (M)	Large Blanket (L)
Measurements with Narrow Border	36 x 42in (91 x 107cm)	51 x 60in (130 x 152cm)	66 x 78in (168 x 198cm)
Yarn Requirements for Narrow Border	390yd (357m)	570yd (521m)	740yd (677m)
Measurements with Wide Border	43 x 49in (109 x 124cm)	58 x 67in (147 x 170cm)	73 x 85in (185 x 216cm)
Yarn Requirements for Wide Border	980yd (896m)	1400yd (1280m)	1800yd (1646m)

Finish your blanket as described for Blanket Without Border. Add the Granny Square Border, using **MC**, **CC1** or any other color and the same hook as for the blocks. With RS facing, join yarn in top right corner (or top left corner for left-handed crochet), turn to WS and work around the entire edge of the blanket. To prevent distortion in the corners, you will change direction in every round.

Rnd 1: (WS) Ch 3 (counts as dc now and throughout), 2 dc in same sp, *[skip 3 sts, 3 dc in next sp] to next corner, (3 dc, ch 2, 3 dc) in corner; repeat 2 more times from *; [skip 3 sts, 3 dc in next sp] to next corner, ending in same sp as beg st; ch 1, hdc in top of beg ch-3 (counts as last corner sp); turn

Rnd 2: (RS) Same as Rnd 1

For Narrow Border: Repeat Rnds 1 - 2 twice more, ending the last corner of Rnd 6 with (ch 2, sl st in top of beg ch-3). Fasten off and weave in the ends.

For Wide Border: Repeat Rnds 1 - 2 six more times, ending the last corner of Rnd 14 with (ch 2, sl st in top of beg ch-3). Fasten off and weave in the ends.

Pattern in corners

Pattern repeat between corners

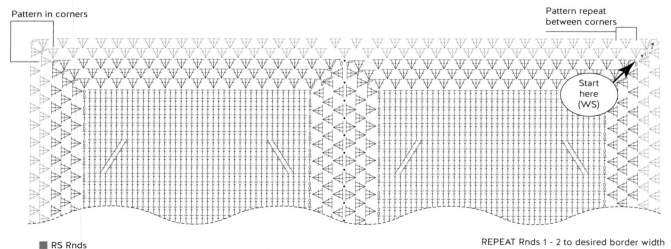

Start here (WS)

REPEAT Rnds 1 - 2 to desired border width

■ RS Rnds
■ WS Rnds
■ Animal Blocks (RS)

Shell Border

· ·

As a decorative, and slightly more complex alternative,
finish your blanket with a pretty shell border.

SIZES AND YARN

Measurements and Yarn	Small Blanket (S)	Medium Blanket (M)	Large Blanket (L)
Measurements with Shell Border	34 x 40in (86 x 102cm)	49 x 58in (124 x 147cm)	64 x 76in (163 x 193cm)
Yarn Requirements for Shell Border	233yd (213m)	335yd (306m)	456yd (417m)

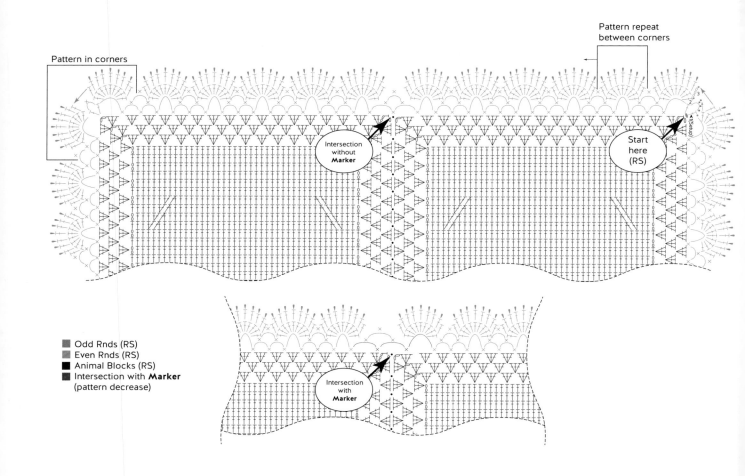

■ Odd Rnds (RS)
■ Even Rnds (RS)
■ Animal Blocks (RS)
■ Intersection with **Marker**
(pattern decrease)

Finish a small, medium or large blanket as described for Blanket Without Border and place **Markers** in intersections indicated in the diagrams (see Blanket Without Border). Add the Shell Border, using **MC** or any other colors and the same hook as for the blocks. With RS facing, begin in top right corner (or top left corner for left-handed crochet) and work around the entire edge of the blanket, removing markers as you go.

Rnd 1: (RS) Setup for Small Blanket (S) only. (Beg dc, ch 5, dc) in corner (fig 1) and work across the top edge without skipping intersection (fig 2) − *[ch 5, skip 3 sts, sc in next sp] to next corner, ch 5, skip 3 sts, (dc, ch 5, dc) in corner**; work down the side edge − ***[ch 5, skip 3 sts, sc in next sp] until 6 sts left before intersection with **Marker**, ch 5, skip 4 sts, sc in next st, ch 5, skip st before and after **Marker** (fig 3), sc in next st, ch 5, skip 4 sts, sc in next sp, [ch 5, skip 3 sts, sc in next sp] to next corner, ch 5, skip 3 sts****, (dc, ch 5, dc) in corner; work across the bottom edge − repeat from * to **; work up the side edge − repeat from *** to ****, join = 146 arches

Rnd 1: (RS) Setup for Medium Blanket (M) only. (Beg dc, ch 5, dc) in corner (fig 1) and work across the top edge − *[ch 5, skip 3 sts, sc in next sp] until 6 sts left before intersection with **Marker**, ch 5, skip 4 sts, sc in next st, ch 5, skip st before and after **Marker** (fig 3), sc in next st, ch 5, skip 4 sts, sc in next sp, repeat once more from *, [ch 5, skip 3 sts, sc in next sp] to next corner, ch 5, skip 3 sts**, (dc, ch 5, dc) in corner***; work down the side edge − repeat from * to ***; work across the bottom edge − repeat from * to ***; work up the side edge − repeat from * to **, join = 212 arches

Rnd 1: (RS) Setup for Large Blanket (L) only. (Beg dc, ch 5, dc) in corner (fig 1) and work across the top edge − *[ch 5, skip 3 sts, sc in next sp] until 6 sts left before intersection with **Marker**, ch 5, skip 4 sts, sc in next st, ch 5, skip st before and after **Marker** (fig 3), sc in next st, ch 5, skip 4 sts, sc in next sp, **[ch 5, skip 3 sts, sc in next sp] to next corner, ch 5, skip 3 sts, (dc, ch 5, dc) in corner***; work down the side edge without skipping intersection (fig 2) − repeat from ** to ***; work across the bottom edge − repeat from * to ***; work up the side edge − [ch 5, skip 3 sts, sc in next sp] to next corner, ch 5, skip 3 sts, join = 290 arches

Continue for all sizes:

Rnd 2: (RS) SI st in next 3 chs of the arch, *9 dc in next arch, sc in next arch, [ch 5, sc in next arch, 9 dc in next arch, sc in next arch] to next corner, ending in corner arch; repeat from * for 2 more times; 9 dc in next arch, sc in next arch, [ch 5, sc in next arch, 9 dc in next arch, sc in next arch] to final 2 arches, ch 5, sc in next arch, 9 dc in last arch, sl st in center of beg arch = 50 (72, 98) shells and 46 (68, 94) arches

Rnd 3: (RS) SI st in dc of next shell, ch 3 (counts as dc), [dc in next st, picot] 7 times, dc in last st of the shell (beg crest made), sc in next arch; *[crest across next shell, sc in next arch] to last shell before corner, crest across shell before corner**, skip sc in corner, crest across next shell, sc in next arch***; repeat 2 more times from * to ***; repeat once from * to **; sl st in top of beg ch-3 = 50 (72, 98) crests

Fasten off and weave in the ends.

(Beg dc, ch5, dc) in corner

Intersection without **Marker**

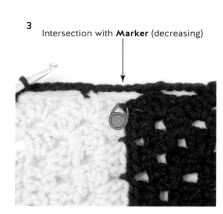

Intersection with **Marker** (decreasing)

One Block Wonders

· ·

If you made an extra block just for fun while testing your gauge, you can turn it into a doll blanket or a wall hanging. I call these small projects One Block Wonders as they are zero-waste gems, wonderful for gift-giving.

DOLL BLANKET

Any finished block can already be used as a doll blanket for up to 18in (45cm) doll, but if you wish to make it slightly larger, you can simply add a few additional granny square rounds working in the pattern as established. For more fun, add tassels across the side and bottom edges (see Finishing Touches). Trim tassels to straighten the edge.

WALL HANGING

To make a wall hanging, you will need a finished animal block, 1 - 2 wooden or bamboo dowel rod(s), and colorful yarn scraps for pom-poms. The dowel rods should be at least 3in (7.5cm) longer than the width of your block.

Thread the tapestry needle with a long piece of **MC** and whipstitch across the top edge of the block, attaching it to the rod. Finish the bottom edge of the block in the same manner using the second rod or add tassels (see Finishing Touches). Trim tassels to straighten the edge.

Using colorful yarn scraps, finish 1 twisted cord and 2 pom-poms as described for the Book Bag. Tie the ends of the cord on each side of the rod and attach pom-poms.

Cushion Cover

· ·

Make your living room feel warm and inviting or simply change the look of a bedroom while keeping your kid's decor sweet and adorable. A cushion cover is easy to remove for washing or switch for a change when you decide.

MATERIALS

- Animal block for front and 280yd (256m) of **MC**
- Animal block or plain block for back and 140yd (128m) of **MC**
- Pillow form insert or cushion – 20 x 20in (51 x 51cm)
- 10 toggle buttons (optional) – 1½in (38mm)

FINISHED MEASUREMENTS

Front: 20 x 27½in (51 x 70cm)

Back: 20 x 20in (51 x 51cm)

Finished Cover: 20 x 20in (51 x 51cm)

Back

Make an animal block (or plain block) with 2 rnds of Granny Square Border and continue working Rnds 3 – 5 in pattern as established for Rnd 2 or until the height of your block measures the same as your cushion. Turn and work in rows across the side edge:

Row 1: (WS) Ch 2 (counts as dc now and throughout), dc in same corner sp, [skip 3 sts, 3 dc in next sp] to final 3 sts, skip 3 sts, 2 dc in last corner sp; turn

Row 2: Ch 2, skip st, 3 dc in next sp, [skip 3 sts, 3 dc in next sp] to final 2 sts, skip st, dc in last st; turn

Row 3: Ch 2, dc in first st, [skip 3 sts, 3 dc in next sp] to final 4 sts, skip 3 sts, 2 dc in last st; turn

Row 4: Same as Row 2

Fasten off, leaving a long tail for sewing.

Join **MC** in the corner on the other side of the block and work across the side edge in the same manner.

NOTE: If you need to adjust the width, you can repeat rows 2 and 3 in pattern as established or omit rows on each side of the shape to fit the width of your cushion.

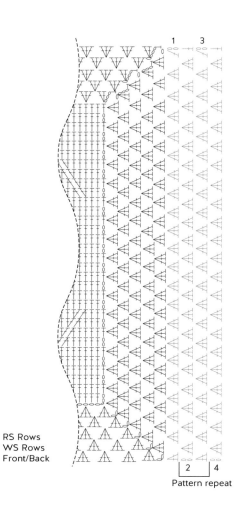

RS Rows
WS Rows
Front/Back

1 3

2 4

Pattern repeat

Front

Same as Back, but repeat Rows 2 – 3 of the side edges in pattern as established until you have 12 rows on each side of the rectangle. You can add or omit rows if alterations are needed. Fasten off and weave in the ends.

Finishing

With RS together, position the back in the center of the front piece and place a **Marker** in each corner to keep pieces in place. Using **MC** tails from the back piece, whipstich across the top and bottom edges, leaving the side edges unstitched (fig 1).

Turn the cover right side out and fold the front flaps onto the back. Place 5 **Markers** evenly spaced along the edge of each front flap to mark closures. Sew a button onto the back piece under each **Marker** or make ties as follows:

With **MC**, ch 15, 3 sl sts across the marked 3-dc group, ch 15 (fig 2). Fasten off, tie a knot on each side of the tie and trim the ends. Make the remaining ties in the same manner, loop the ties through the stitches of the back piece and tie bows.

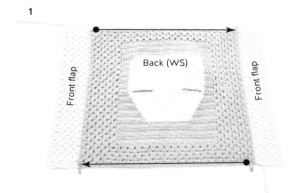

Book Bag and Backpack

Bring your book to the beach in a cute backpack or make a colorful book bag to inspire your kids for reading before bed. This bag and backpack are finished in the same manner using 2 blocks, but the cords are attached differently for each style.

MATERIALS

- Animal block for front
- Animal block or plain block for back
- 4 colors of choice for pom-poms – 40yd (37m) of each
- 2 colors of choice for cords – 14yd (13m) of each color for book bag or 20yd (18m) of each color for backpack

FINISHED MEASUREMENTS

15 x 18½in (38 x 47cm)

Book Bag / Backpack

Use 1 animal block for the front and 1 animal or plain block for the back. With WS together, join these 2 blocks across the side and bottom edges, using your favorite method (see Joining Blocks). Leave the top edge open. Join **MC** in corner space between the joined blocks and work around the top edge as follows: [Ch 2, 2 dc in same sp, skip 3 sts, sl st in next sp] around. Fasten off and weave in the ends.

Finishing

Make 2 twisted cords by using 2 lengths of 2 different colors for each cord – 120in (305cm) for a book bag or 180in (457cm) for a backpack. Also, prepare 4 pom-poms using different colors of yarn (see Finishing Touches).

To finish a book bag, pull the cords through the top corners (fig 1) and attach pom-poms to each end. Tie the cords around the back of a chair or onto the footer side of a bed frame and drop in your favorite book.

For the backpack, attach 2 twisted cords as follows:

First cord: Begin and end in top left corner, weaving the cord through the spaces below the edging round. You should have 2 long ends on the left (fig 2).

Second cord: Begin and end on the right, weaving the cord through the spaces below the first cord. You should have 2 long ends on the right (fig 2).

Pull one of the left ends through the bottom left corner of the backpack from front to back and pull the second end through the same corner but from back to front (fig 3). Finish the right side in the same manner and attach pom-poms to each end. Pull the cords on each side to gather the top edge and tie the bottom end to adjust the length of the shoulder straps.

SAFETY NOTE: Adult supervision is advised for handmade items with cords, tassels and pom-poms when they are used by small children.

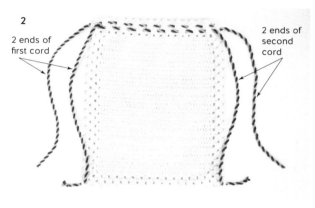

2 ends of first cord

2 ends of second cord

Tip

· · · · · · · · · · · · · · · ·

For a change, and to add more fun, use a different animal block for the back and the front.

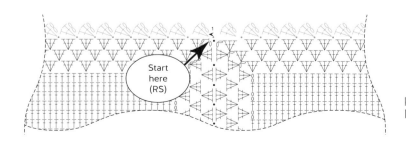

Start here (RS)

Edging (RS)
Front/Back

Toy Storage Bag

Have fun cleaning up the play room with your little one! This simple yet adorable tote bag will fit a load of toys to help you organize your room. It's also a great project for using up yarn scraps so nothing goes to waste.

MATERIALS

- 2 animal blocks (1 for front and 1 for back)
- A color of choice or yarn scraps for borders – 900yd (823m)
- A color of choice for 2 pom-poms – 80yd (73m)
- 2 colors of choice for cords – 14yd (13m) of each color

FINISHED MEASUREMENTS

26 x 32½in (66 x 82.5cm)

Back and Front

Make 1 back and 1 front. Finish an animal block with 2 rounds of Granny Square Border and continue working Rnds 3 – 15 in pattern as established for Rnd 2. Keep changing the direction of your work in every round to prevent distortion in the corners. You can work these 15 rounds of Granny Square Border using any yarn color you like or change colors in every round.

Finishing

With WS together, join the back and front pieces across the side and bottom edges, using your favorite method (see Joining Blocks). Leave the top edge open. With RS facing, join yarn in corner space of the front piece and work around the top edge of the bag as follows:

Rnd 1: Ch 3 (counts as dc now and throughout), 2 dc in same sp, *[skip 3 sts, 3 dc in next sp] 28 times, skip 3 sts, 3 dc in next ch-1 sp before join**; skip join, 3 dc in next ch-1 sp of the back piece, repeat from * to **; sl st in top of beg ch-3 = 30 groups of 3-dc

Rnds 2 – 3: Ch 3, 2 dc in same sp, [skip 3 sts, 3 dc in next sp] around; sl st in top of beg ch-3 = 60 groups of 3-dc

Rnd 4: Ch 1 (does not count as a st), sc in same sp, ch 5, skip 3 sts, sc in next sp, [ch 5, skip 3 sts, sc in next sp] to final 3 sts; ch 2, skip 3 sts, dc in beg st (counts as last arch) = 60 arches

Rnd 5: Skip dc-sp, 9 dc in next arch, sc in next arch, [ch 5, sc in next arch, 9 dc in next arch, sc in next arch] around, ending in last arch; ch 2, skip 2 chs of next arch, dc in last dc (counts as last arch) = 20 shells and 20 arches

Rnd 6: [Crest across next shell, sc in next arch] around, ending the last repeat with sl st = 20 crests

Fasten off and weave in the ends. Make 1 twisted cord by using 2 lengths of 2 different colors – 240in (610cm) and prepare 2 pom-poms using colors of your choice (see Finishing Touches). Weave the cord through the spaces below the large shells and attach a pom-pom to each end. Fill the tote bag with toys, pull the cords to gather the top edge and tie it into a bow.

Safety Note

. . . .

Adult supervision is advised for handmade items with cords, tassels and pom-poms when they are used by small children.

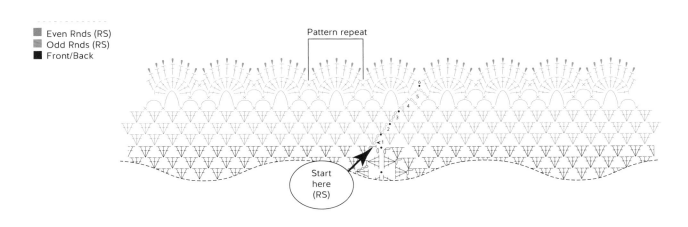

■ Even Rnds (RS)
■ Odd Rnds (RS)
■ Front/Back

Pattern repeat

Start here (RS)

Useful Information

· · · · · · · · · · ·

TERMINOLOGY

The patterns featured in this book are written using abbreviations in American terms. You can use the comparison chart below to convert the patterns to British terminology if needed.

Abbreviation	Symbol	American (US Term)	British (UK) Term
ch	⬭	Chain	Chain
sl st	●	Slip stitch	Slip stitch
sc	✕	Single crochet	Double crochet
hdc	T	Half double crochet	Half treble crochet
dc	⊤	Double crochet	Treble crochet
tr	⊤	Treble crochet	Double treble crochet
		Skip	Miss
		Gauge	Tension

ABBREVIATIONS

This table explains all of the standard abbreviations and symbols used in this book.

Abbreviation	Symbol	Description in American (US) Terms
arch	 ⌒	Arch is a group of 5 chains; when working in the arch, insert the hook under the chains (and not into a specific chain)
beg		Begin(ning)
beg PC		Beginning popcorn stitch – Ch 3 (counts as dc), 4 dc in same st, remove the hook from the loop and insert it from front to back through the top of beg ch-3, replace the loop onto the hook (from the last dc) and pull it through
beg dc		Beginning (standing) double crochet – Make a slipknot and keep the loop on the hook, yo, insert the hook through the stitch and complete dc as normal
beg sc		Beginning (standing) single crochet – Make a slipknot and keep the loop on the hook, insert the hook through the stitch and complete sc as normal
BLO		Back loop only – Work through the back loop only when indicated
bpdc	RS WS 	Back post double crochet – Yo, insert the hook from back to front to back around the post of the stitch, yo and pull up a loop, [yo and pull yarn through 2 loops on the hook] 2 times

Abbreviation	Symbol	Description in American (US) Terms
CC		Contrasting color (exact one will be indicated by a number)
ch(s)	⬭	Chain(s) – Yo and pull through the loop on the hook
ch-		Indicates a number of chains or spaces previously made (example: ch-2 sp)
cm		Centimeter(s)
crest		Crest is a combination of stitches worked across the shell – Dc in first st of the shell, [dc in next st, picot] 7 times, dc in last st = 9 dc and 7 picots
dc		Double crochet – Yo, insert the hook in stitch, yo and pull up a loop, [yo and pull through 2 loops on the hook] 2 times
dc2(3)tog		Double crochet 2 (3) together (decrease) – [Yo, insert the hook in next stitch, yo and pull up a loop, yo and pull through 2 loops on the hook] 2(3) times, yo and pull through all loops on the hook
		2 (3) dc in same stitch or space as indicated in the pattern
dc-lp(s)		Double crochet loop(s) – Loop st created while working dc (see Special Stitches)
		2 dc-lps in same stitch
	→ ➤	Direction indicators
fasten off		Cut working yarn, draw the end through the loop on the hook and pull up tight
FLO		Front loop only – Work through the front loop only when indicated
fpdc	RS WS	Front post double crochet – Yo, insert the hook from front to back to front around the post of the stitch, yo and pull up a loop, [yo and pull yarn through 2 loops on the hook] 2 times
fpsc		Front post single crochet – Insert the hook from front to back to front around the post of the stitch, yo and pull up a loop, yo and pull yarn through 2 loops on hook
hdc		Half double crochet – Yo, insert the hook in stitch, yo and pull up a loop, yo and pull through all loops on the hook
in		Inch(es)
join		Sl st in top of the first stitch, not a chain
m		Meter(s)
	◎	Magic ring or ch-3 circle
MC		Main color
PC		Popcorn stitch – 5 dc into same stitch, remove the hook from the loop and insert it from front to back through the top of the first dc, replace the loop onto the hook (from the last dc) and pull it through

Abbreviation	Symbol	Description in American (US) Terms
picot	❗	Picot – Ch 3, insert the hook through the base of the previously made stitch, yo and pull through all loops on the hook
Rnd(s)		Round(s) – Work in spiral or join the rounds, as indicated in the pattern
Row(s)		Row(s) – Turn after finishing each row, as indicated in the pattern
RS		Right side (front side of the item)
rsc	⊼	Reverse single crochet (crab stitch) – Insert the hook in stitch to the right from front to back, yo and pull it through, yo and pull through all loops on the hook (For left-handed crochet, insert the hook in stitch to the left instead of right)
sc	✕	Single crochet – Insert the hook in stitch, yo and pull up a loop, yo and pull through all loops on the hook
sc3tog	⋈	Single crochet 3 together (decrease) – [Insert the hook in next stitch, yo and pull up a loop] 3 times, yo and pull through all loops on the hook
	⋉ ⋈	2 (3) sc in same stitch or space
		Seam
shell		Shell is a group of 9 dc (or fewer) worked in same stitch or space as indicated in the pattern
sl st	●	Slip stitch – Insert the hook in stitch, yo and pull through the stitch and loop on the hook
sp		Space is a gap created by one or more chains; it might also be a space between two stitches or groups of stitches. Insert the hook into a chain space or in a space between stitches (not a specific chain or stitch)
st(s)		Stitch(es)
tr	⟊	Treble crochet – Yo twice, insert the hook in stitch, yo and pull up a loop, [yo and pull through 2 loops] 3 times
WS		Wrong side (back side of the item)
x-dc	⋉	Cross double crochet - Skip st, dc in next st, dc in skipped st
yd		Yard(s)
yo		Yarn over
		Yarn tail left for sewing
[ ]		Work the instructions written within brackets as many times as indicated after brackets
( )		Parentheses are used in explanations or to indicate a group of stitches
* or **		Asterisks are used as reference marks
=		Equal sign indicates the total stitch count at the end of the row/rnd

Special Stitches

SEWING STITCHES

When sewing, take extra care pulling the needle along the top layer of the fabric (not all the way through) to prevent contrasting color yarn from showing on the back of the work (figs 1 - 3).

Backstitch

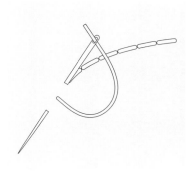

Chain stitch

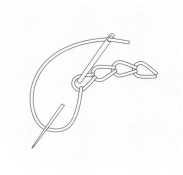

Whipstitch

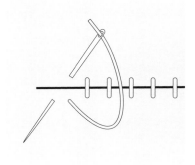

CROCHET STITCHES

The loops in the Lion and Sheep Blocks are created in the middle of dc stitches and they appear on the back of the work, so you will be working on the WS to create loops on RS of your block.

Double crochet loop (dc-lp) – Yo and hold the yarn over your index finger. Insert the hook in st and pass it over and behind the yarn to catch the far side of the working yarn (fig 4). Pull both strands through the stitch; adjust the size of the loop to fit your finger circumference loosely and release the loop off of your finger; yo and pull through the double-wrap just made and yo from the beginning (fig 5), yo and complete dc as usual. Dc-lp is completed with a loop on the back of the work.

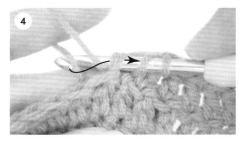

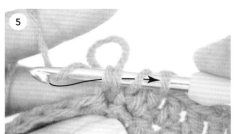

BUTTERFLY-BOBBINS

To make a butterfly-bobbin, take the end from a yarn skein, wrap it around your thumb and bring across your palm over towards your pinkie. Wrap yarn around your pinkie and bring it back to your thumb creating an 8-shaped path. Continue wrapping in the same motion to make a thick yarn bundle (fig 6). Remove the bundle off of your hand, cut yarn and secure the end around the center (fig 7). Pull the end from the beginning to crochet.

CHANGING COLORS

Regular color change: Leave the dc before the color change unfinished, with 2 loops on the hook. Drop the working yarn off of your index finger and pick up the new color, pulling it through the remaining loops on the hook (fig 8). The stitch is now completed with the new color on the hook.

Decreasing color change: Leave the dc2tog before the color change unfinished, with 3 loops on the hook. Drop the working yarn off of your index finger and pick up the new color, pulling it through the remaining loops on the hook (fig 9). The decrease stitch is now completed with the new color on the hook.

INTARSIA

Colorwork in this book is done using the Intarsia colorwork technique that allows changing colors without carrying yarn horizontally through the stitches. Each section of color has its own working yarn that moves from row to row as you crochet, creating vertical floats on the back of the work. Since each section of color is worked using an individual yarn source, you will need to prepare some butterfly-bobbins that you will use in different color sections along with the original skein or ball of yarn for larger sections (fig 10). The patterns will specify which source of yarn to use when you are setting up the first row of colorwork.

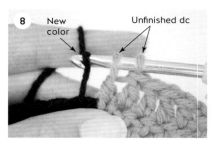

New color • Unfinished dc

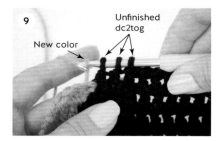

Unfinished dc2tog • New color

Yarn ball • Butterfly-bobbin • Yarn skein

Joining Blocks

· · · · · · · · · · · ·

Here are 4 different ways of joining granny square blocks: Whipstitch Through FLO, Mattress Stitch (Invisible), Slip Stitch Through BLO and Join-As-You-Go (JAYGO). Choose a joining method that suits your skill level or try different methods for different projects for a challenge. Depending on the joining method and your project, you can finish the animal faces on your blocks before or after joining.

WHIPSTITCH THROUGH FLO

Finish all blocks required for your project (including 3 rounds of Granny Square Border as in Penguin Block) and sew the facial features onto each block. Position the blocks based on your project layout and sew them together as follows: Thread the tapestry needle with **MC** and whipstitch from corner to corner through the corresponding stitches of 2 blocks, inserting the needle through FLO. Finish off and weave in the end. Repeat, sewing in the same manner, across the corresponding edges (figs 11 and 12).

MATTRESS STITCH (INVISIBLE)

Finish all blocks required for your project (including 3 rounds of Granny Square Border as in Penguin Block) and sew the facial features onto each block. Position the blocks based on your project layout and sew them together as follows: Thread the tapestry needle with **MC** and sew from corner to corner through the corresponding stitches of 2 blocks – insert the needle from back to front through the ch in corner of the left block, then through the ch in corner of the right block; *insert the needle from back to front under both loops of next st on the left, then through the next st on the right; repeat from * ending in corner chs. Finish off and weave in the end. Repeat sewing in the same manner across the corresponding edges (figs 13 - 15).

SLIP STITCH THROUGH BLO

Finish all blocks required for your project (including 3 rounds of Granny Square Border as in Penguin Block) and sew the facial features onto each block. Position the blocks as you like, based on your project layout and join them together using **MC** and a 5mm (H) hook as follows: Make a slipknot and keep the loop on the hook; insert the hook from front to back through the corner chs of both blocks and complete sl st; *sl st in next st of both pieces at the same time working through BLO; repeat from * ending in corner chs. Finish off and weave in the ends. Repeat joining in the same manner across the corresponding edges (figs 16 - 18).

JOIN-AS-YOU-GO (JAYGO)

Finish your first block and sew the facial features onto the block. For all the remaining blocks required for your project, sew the facial features after the joining round (Rnd 3 of Granny Square Border as in Penguin Block). Work the joining rnd as follows: Begin the rnd as described and work to the corner where you need to start joining; work in corner – 3 dc, ch 1, sl st into corresponding corner of the previously made block, ch 1, 3 dc in same corner; *skip 3 sts, 3 dc in next sp, sl st into corresponding sp of the previously made block; repeat from * to next corner. Continue to work around the remaining sides of the block in pattern as established, ending the rnd as described in the pattern (figs 19 - 21).

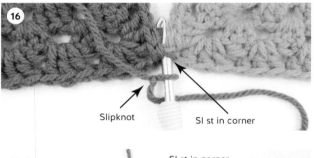

Slipknot   Sl st in corner

Sl st in corner

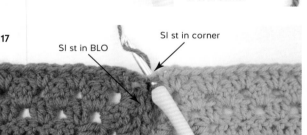

Sl st in BLO   Sl st in corner

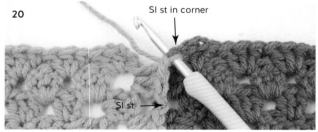

Sl st in corner

Sl st

Finishing Touches

· · · · · · · · · · · · · ·

POM-POM

To make a pom-pom, wrap yarn 120 times loosely around 4 fingers or use a 3¹/₂in (9cm) piece of cardboard. Slide the wrapped bundle off of your fingers and tie firmly around the center with another long piece of yarn. Cut all the loops around and trim the pom-pom to create a nice round shape (fig 22).

TASSEL

To make a tassel, wrap yarn 5 times loosely around 4 fingers or use a 3¹/₂in (9cm) piece of cardboard. Cut the wraps on 1 side and fold the yarn bundle in half. Insert the hook through the stitches of the block and pull it through, creating a loop. Pull the yarn ends through the loop and tighten them (fig 23). Trim the ends.

OPPOSITE SIDE OF FOUNDATION CHAIN

Complete all of the required stitches, working in each chain across the foundation chain and place the increase stitches in the last chain. Rotate your work and crochet along the bottom loops of the foundation chain (fig 24).

DUO COLORED TWISTED CORD

Cut 2 lengths of each yarn color, fold them in half and loop these 2 bundles in the middle. Attach one side of the yarn bundle to a door knob and twist the cord very tightly in the same direction, applying consistent tension. Fold the twisted rope in half where 2 colors meet and bring their ends together. Release the folded end and let it spin. Tie a knot to secure the ends (figs 25 - 27).

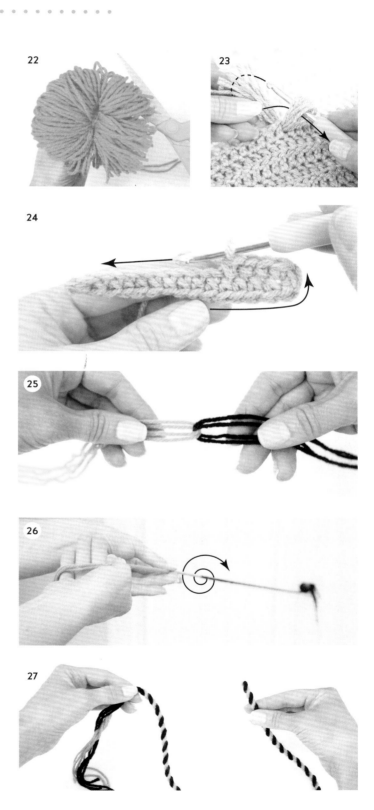

About the Author

Hi! I am a Canadian fiber artist, pattern designer and author. Coming from a family of textile engineers, my childhood was filled with fabrics and yarns from the time I was born. Thus, needlecrafting has always felt natural to me. While I enjoy all kinds of textile art, there's a special place in my heart for crocheting and it will always be my first love.

I learned to sew, knit and crochet at a very young age and I enjoy sharing my passion for fiber art through my designs inspired by animals and nature. My happy place is where fabric and yarn meet fun!

I hope you will enjoy making animal blocks from this book as much as I enjoyed designing them. Please check out my previous books as well – *Crochet Animal Rugs* and *Crochet Animal Slippers*.

Thanks

I would like to thank Yarnspirations for providing their beautiful Red Heart Super Saver yarn that allowed us to test all of the animal blocks and projects from this book! I am forever grateful to our testing team members and I appreciate the time they spent testing my patterns, checking all the yarn requirements and proofreading – Cheryl McNichols, Lenore Cartlidge, Ryan Nicole Hazeltine, Helen Hamilton and Cynthia Fuller.

Suppliers

Recommended Yarn
Red Heart Super Saver Yarn
Bernat Super Value Yarn
Bernat Premium Yarn
Yarnspirations.com

General Yarn
Canada – Canada.michaels.com
USA – Joann.com
UK – Hobbycraft.co.uk
Worldwide – Lovecrafts.com

Additional Supplies
Canada – Walmart.ca
USA – Walmart.com
Australia and New Zealand – Spotlightstores.com
Worldwide – Amazon.com

Index

ISBN-13: 9781446309216 paperback
ISBN-13: 9781446381632 EPUB
ISBN-13: 9781446381625 PDF

This book has been printed on paper from approved
suppliers and made from pulp from sustainable sources.

FSC
www.fsc.org

MIX
Paper from
responsible sources
FSC® C002375

Printed in the UK by Buxton Press for:
David and Charles, Ltd
Suite A, Tourism House, Pynes Hill, Exeter, EX2 5WS

10 9 8 7 6 5 4 3 2 1

Publishing Director: Ame Verso
Managing Editor: Jeni Chown
Project Editor: Sam Winkler
Head of Design: Anna Wade
Senior Designer: Sam Staddon
Designer: Blanche Williams
Pre-press Designer: Ali Stark
Art Direction: Prudence Rogers
Photography: Jason Jenkins
Production Manager: Beverley Richardson

David and Charles publishes high-quality books on
a wide range of subjects. For more information visit
www.davidandcharles.com.

Share your makes with us on social media using
#dandcbooks and follow us on Facebook and Instagram
by searching for @dandcbooks.

Layout of the digital edition of this book may vary
depending on reader hardware and display settings.